THE COMMITMENT

<u>ALSO BY NICK BUNICK</u>

IN GOD'S TRUTH

TRANSITIONS OF THE SOUL

TIME FOR TRUTH...A NEW BEGINNING

THE MESSENGERS

(DESCRIPTIONS OF THE ABOVE BOOKS CAN BE FOUND ON THE LAST PAGE OF THIS BOOK)

THE COMMITMENT

(THE TRUE STORY)

By

Nick Bunick

Skywin LLC

P.O. Box 2222

Lake Oswego, Oregon 97035

Bunick, Nick.

The Commitment/Nick Bunick.

1st edition, June 2011

ISBN-10 1461177553
ISBN-13 978-1461177555
BISAC: Religion / Spirituality
Skywin,
P.O. Box 2222
Lake Oswego, Oregon 97035

The cover of The Commitment is provided through the courtesy of www.public-domain-image.com

CONTENTS

Introduction

The Commitment will provide you with the details of the true lives of Jeshua (Jesus) and Paul beyond anything that has ever been written before.

You will discover exactly what Jeshua and Paul looked like, what they wore, the food they ate, how they entertained themselves, what were their goals and dreams, what were their motivations....how they dealt with the challenges in their lives and experience with them the decisions they made that impacted the lives of billions of people throughout history, and even today.

You will read teachings and messages from Jeshua never seen before. You will walk with them through the streets of Jerusalem... along the Sea of Galilee... in the market place and the bazaar where they shopped and dined... and you will be given an understanding of their lives, their aspirations and the events that influenced their decisions in details that will change your life and provide you THE TRUE STORY.

Please allow me to explain to you how I was able to provide you

this extraordinary information. It began in the latter part of the 20th century, when a friend persuaded me to visit with a psychic. I was reluctant to do so, for I did not believe in psychics at that time. It was totally adverse to my background. I had been born and raised in one of the poorest cities in the country; a suburb of Boston called Chelsea, and attended college on a football scholarship at the University of Florida.

I then spent a period of time in the US Army as second in command of 1700 men in an elite organization called Special Troops. Years later I found myself living the American dream, with a loving family and a nice home and owned three successful small companies. I had no formal religion, (still do not), and certainly would never have been described as a "new age" person.

The experience with the psychic, Duane Berry, was the beginning of an incredible journey I have been on. He knew everything about my life, past, present and future. He told me there would come a time when I would be speaking in front of thousands of people in live audiences and millions on radio and television, which all eventually happened. He said it would have to do with "The time I walked with the master 2000 years ago".

After I had this message repeated to me by other seers, I reluctantly agreed to allow a professional hypnotist, Julia Ingram, to age regress me to a past life. Over a period of six months of taped sessions, I discovered I had the entire memory of the Apostle Paul. All of these experiences were captured in detail in the New York Times best seller, The Messengers, authored by Gary Hardin and myself, Nick Bunick, which led me to indeed speak in front of thousands of people in live audiences and millions on radio and television, as the psychic, Duane Berry had told me I would.

Miracles began to happen all around me which I have written about in other books. For now, I don't want to stray from what I feel is so important for you to know as to what is the source of the information in *The Commitment* and why indeed, it is **The True Story**.

I discovered that indeed every one of us have angels and spirit guides in our lives. I was given the gift of having access to the memory of Paul without having to go into hypnotic regression. I was also given the gift of being able to channel information in writing and provided with writing skills from the spirit world that were extraordinary and more profound than I otherwise would have not have had. Lastly, "spirit" also gave me the gift of claircognizance, in which they provide information into my mind and memory not previously known by me.

All of these factors above... the accessing through my soul mind the memory of Paul... channeled writings from the "spirit" world... and "spirit" providing me the information through claircognizance created the words found in *The Commitment.*

Please join me in this journey of two thousand years ago. I promise you, it will change your life forever.

Nick Bunick

Chapter 1
The City

The young man pressed his weight against the front door of his house. He heard the familiar scraping sound of wood against worn wood. Sunlight flooded onto the stone tiles of the kitchen floor as he gently stepped into the pleasant front yard, consuming a deep breath of the fresh summer morning air. Saul loved this time of day. He could feel the beginning of the gentle heat emanating from the rising sun absorbing the early morning dew.

He stepped forward in his bare feet, feeling the sensation of the dampness of the red clay mixed with the warm surface of the ground. He wished he could touch some magic button, which would allow the entire day of this gentle warmth that he thought of as a marriage between the earlier chilled darkness of evening and the coming heat of the sun filled day.

He casually walked over to the bench that had been built by his

Landlord years ago, which commanded a view of the exciting city below. His heart sang with joy as his vision glanced from left to right, first viewing the immense magnificent Great Temple with the encompassing Holy Great Wall below him to his left, and then further down the hillside towards the center, where the extraordinary, exciting city, known as the lower city, flattened out to a myriad of activities. He could barely make out the central market place, the bazaar, where thousands would visit before the day had been completed.

His eyes followed the narrow streets connecting the market place to thousands of homes in all four directions, some moving up the hill towards him, known as the upper city, to the larger and more luxurious homes. Other roads lead away from the bazaar to the poorer neighborhoods in the opposite direction from his beloved upper city.

The soon to be steaming, bustling market place of downtown was located in the heart of this great city. The winding, narrow streets as well as the houses on the hillside led from all directions to the commercial center of the city, which featured hundreds of retail shops, restaurants, taverns, offices of money lenders, tailor shops, bakeries, shoe makers, tent makers, artisans and artists, wine shops, public baths and sellers of the products of the carpet and rug weavers.

"Oh Jerusalem, you beautiful lady," he gently whispered, "How I do love you. Thank you dear God for letting me be a part of it." Saul loved this magical city, the city of rolling hills, large wealthy homes built on the higher ground, and crowded, dirty, noisy, winding streets in the lower city leading into the central market place. Jerusalem was a city partially built on a hill, a city of marble, stone, domes, spires, narrow cobblestone streets, and alleys. It was a city with Roman aqueducts, market places, gardens, villas, red earth, gravel paths and gray stone walls.

Saul could hear the front door opening behind him. He glanced over his shoulder, as Jocelyn, the wife of the landlord, stood partially in the doorway, with one hand over her brow, shielding the sunlight from her eyes. "Saul, would you like something to eat? I am cooking some white fish that I can serve with some eggs and pastries." Saul stood up and turned to face her. He liked this quiet, gentle woman that was half Jewish and half Persian. Her morning robe of a light gray soft fabric covered her ample bosom and stopped just below the leather straps of her shoes. Her kind, gentle brown eyes were slightly wide, waiting for his response, in contrast to the smooth olive color skin of her face.

Saul stretched his youthful body, still wearing his loose fitting garment that he had worn to bed, allowing the sleeves to fall down to his elbows, revealing the wiry, muscular arms of an athlete. Saul smiled. "No, thank you Jocelyn. I am going to meet some friends for breakfast at the bazaar. But thank you for the offer." Jocelyn responded "Oh, too bad, I had a special price for you today."

Both of them gently laughed as Jocelyn turned back into the house. Saul once again turned his body and eyes to the city that lay before him. Still stretching his graceful body, he glanced and admired the expensive villas that sat alongside of and above his rented house, on the hillside overlooking the city.

They were made of white marble adorned with columns, statues, fountains, atriums, and gardens. These properties were enclosed in white stone walls with gates of iron and the houses were surrounded by sycamore, carob, pine and palm trees.

"Oh you beautiful lady," he sighed, "I would marry you tomorrow, if not for your thousands of unruly children, that I do not want to be a father to."

Chapter 2
The Childhood

It had been five exciting years since Saul had left his home, on the outskirts of the city of Tarsus, in the region of Celesia. His father had built an extravagant estate on the outskirts of the city of Saul's birthplace. Although he had grown up in luxury, Saul did not have many fond memories of his youth. He had actually spent more time with his tutors, then he had with his parents. Saul's father was a very austere man, a man of few words, who showed little affection to those around him. Saul's sister was considerably older than him and had moved to another region with her husband when he was still a child.

Saul was indifferent to the wealth that he had been exposed to as a child, but he had been grateful for one decision that his father had made. Tarsus was a city which was occupied by the Romans, as was Jerusalem and a large part of the Holy Land. Before Saul had been

born, his father had made the decision that his family would be Roman citizens.

There were three ways in which a Jewish family could become a citizen of Rome, one of them a result of having been a slave in Rome under the rule of Pompei, who sixty-five years before Saul was born, had granted the Jews Roman citizenship along with their freedom. A second way was to perform some extraordinary feat that was beneficial to the Romans, where they in turn would show their appreciation by rewarding you with citizenship. His father had selected the third way, which was to purchase Roman citizenship by paying a large sum of money to the Roman Empire.

It was later while living in the Holy Land that Saul would utilize the benefits of being a Roman citizen. Even though Jerusalem, at first was a city that was foreign to him, Saul felt security by having Roman citizenship, an advantage in which the Jews and other citizens of Jerusalem did not have. If he were to be accused of a crime, he had the right to demand trial by a Roman court, even if the crime being accused of, and those making the accusations, took place outside of Rome.

Here in Jerusalem, he could see the influence of the Roman Empire all around him. Many of the roads were cobblestone, and built by the Romans to allow for the movement of their horses and carts.

Often times, you could hear the iron tapped shoes of the boots of the Roman soldiers, clicking in unison as they marched or trotted through the narrow streets. The sight of Roman soldiers did not disturb Saul. Had he not grown up as a child looking upon the soldiers as his protectors?

Most of Saul's daytime in Tarsus was spent in studying with his tutors. They had taught him many wonderful things, which challenged his intellect. He had learned the ability to speak not only in the language of the Romans as well as Greek, but also to be totally fluent in the Hebrew language which was akin to Aramaic, which he would find necessary to use later in life in his newly adopted Jerusalem.

When he was not studying during the day, he would spend his time chasing the sheep over the hills of his father's property, or swimming in the lake a short distance from the main residence. He could remember as a child lying on his back along the grassy hillsides and open meadows of the property, staring upwards, watching as the sun would move across the beautiful blue sky that hovered above him.

He had been taught that the sky was a huge plate that separated the earth from the heavens and in the daytime the sun and the clouds would travel underneath this plate. It was then replaced by a myriad of stars and the moon, which substituted the darkness for the brightness of the sun. He often wondered why the moon would take different shapes, sometimes round and full, shining like a brilliant copper circle and other times only showing slivers of itself. He often asked himself, how this could be possible, and what the purpose of God was changing the shape of the moon, other than for the entertainment of those who lived below the heavens.

Saul would often try to use his imagination as to what the heavens must be like on the other side of the "plate". Were there

lakes and green rolling hills and beautiful flowers and trees also found in heaven? Were there mountain ranges like those that surrounded Tarsus, and rivers like the majestic Cyndus, which traveled between the gorges in the mountains, through his home land all the way to the ocean? Were rivers of that nature also to be found in heaven?

Saul remembered the conversation that he had once had with one of his religious tutors. He had asked the man these same questions that he often pondered over during those quiet moments lying in his father's meadows, and the Rabbi had responded "Why must you know these things Paulus? You ask questions that have no value to your soul or to your body. The answers to these questions are in the realm of God, and surely there will come a time when you yourself will know the answers to these questions, as a personal witness."

But Saul was not satisfied with those responses. His curious and intellectual mind, even though being that of a child, realized that the Rabbi did not know the answers. But that didn't mean that Saul would not someday discover the truth to those questions that so intrigued him. Even at a very early age, Saul had ambitions to someday live in the Holy Land, in the heart of Judaism, in the city of Jerusalem, where he would be able to meet with others and have exciting discussions with some of the great minds of those people who were experts regarding the laws of God, as well as in the Judaic religion. Yes indeed, someday Saul was determined that he would make that journey, and hopefully, while he was still a young man.

Saul was grateful for having the quality of education that was made available to him. His father, being the austere man that he was, would not let Paul attend public school, or for that matter private school, where he would be taught at the same pace as other students. Instead, the very finest teachers were made available to him, allowing his father to believe that he was a caring and gentle parent rather than the indifferent, ungiving and unemotional person that he was.

Saul's mother, although more sensitive than his father, still held back her feelings, as well as her opinions. She was very frightened of his father, and suppressed her feelings as well as subordinated all authority to her husband. Deep in her heart she longed to hold the precious child, to cuddle him and give him her love, but she knew this display of emotion would be frowned upon greatly by her husband, and be prevented from happening. Saul observed at an early age, that marriage was an unpleasant experience and one that he was determined to avoid.

Tarsus was located on a plain surrounded by the Tarsus Mountains on its north and the mountains of Amanus in the west, and the river Cyndus flowed from the Tarsus Mountains, through a gorge and eventually into the Great Sea which some day would be renamed the Mediterranean. Tarsus itself was seven miles from the sea. Paul was allowed to frequently visit the actual interior of the city of Tarsus, although not on a daily basis.

The city was a great learning center, which included philosophers, poets and many scholars. Approximately three hundred years earlier, Alexander the Great had conquered the area of Celesia. This had allowed a complete Hellenistic influencing of Tarsus several hundred years prior to the Roman occupation.

As a child, as Paul walked through the streets of Tarsus with his male chaperone, he was wide eyed and intrigued with the incredible sights before him. Once he had visited the city during the Roman holiday of Saturnalia and was fascinated with the hundreds of Roman centurions, wearing their Roman visors, with Roman banners and bronze eagles waving in the breeze. The people of Tarsus considered the Romans as fair administrators of their region who believed in law and order in government.

The Roman legionnaires looked authoritative in their iron shod shoes and their short swords pressed against their hips. The city of Tarsus had been tremendously influenced by Roman occupation which included places of entertainment and commercial activities designed to attract the spending of the copper and shekel coins of currency, and the many stores of money brokers to accommodate them. The streets were filled with excitement from the shops of the cabinet makers, cosmetic manufacturers, dancing pigs, sports arenas, brothels, and many other enterprising activities.

On a busy day along the port that had been created on the Cyndus River, the streets were filled with sailors, fishermen, two wheeled wagons and the sounds of shouts of many languages. On the interior, streets could be found with students, doctors, actors, farmers, merchants, acrobats and gladiators. What an incredible contrast for this inquisitive youngster to experience, as opposed to the expansive quiet rolling hills surrounding the beautiful estate of his wealthy parents.

Paul identified more with the city then he did with the countryside. He once said to his favorite tutor with whom he often confided "My heart longs to be in the city. My education is of no value to me in the countryside, unless I choose to try to educate the sheep." Astoncs, Paul's tutor, laughed and responded "Oh Paulus, if your knowledge is as keen as your sense of humor, you surely will become the greatest teacher that the sheep have ever been exposed to. However, I don't think that is what your father has in mind."

"But he seems so protective of me, in not letting me visit the city more often. What is my future?" Paul asked, with an obvious sadness in his voice. The tutor hesitated, studying Paul with great intensity. He felt compassion for the young teenager, realizing that he did not have a close relationship with his parents and that he was almost living in isolation on the estate, with exception of the company of his educated tutors and the servants.

After much hesitation, Astoncs responded, "It's possible that your father is considering allowing you to go to the Holy Land. I suggest that when your education is finished, ask him Permission to do so, and you may be surprised at his response."

Paul felt an immediate rush of excitement go through his young body. "Oh, if only that is true, then I am indeed grateful for the wonderful words of wisdom that you have taught me, my dear teacher, and I in turn will use them to their fullest value in the Holy Land. I will keep this information to myself, but I'm so grateful for your sharing these thoughts."

The time had come following his eighteenth birthday that Paul had made the decision to ask his father's permission to move to the Holy Land. That morning, while he walked along the red gravel foot path surrounded by dense grass and through the lush gardens, he re-

hearsed in his mind how he would approach his father.

Finally, when he was satisfied with the words that he would use, he entered his home through the immense bronze entry doors, passed the central atrium with its white marble walls and white marble floors and quietly walked into the library, where he knew his father would be studying, looking through manuscripts.

The ceiling of the library were plastered and decorated in rosettes of gold and blue. There were many bookshelves filled with manuscripts of various sizes and shapes. His father was sitting in a large chair made of a combination of dark ebony and teak. He was wearing a loose fitting white tunic covered with a gold girdle over his lean frame, and an embroidered jeweled white skull cap.

He looked up when he heard Paul approach him, with an austere challenging look on his face, which had an expression as if to ask, "Why are you bothering me?" His father's greatest interest in life was his scholarly pursuits and the management of his assets and his estate. He felt he had very little in common trying to deal with the interests and personalities of children.

Was he not taking care of his fatherly responsibilities by providing his son with an outstanding education as well as the excellent living conditions that he had created on his estate? He knew in his discussions with the tutors of Paul, that his son was very bright and had done exceptionally well in his studies, and obviously he was in good health. He felt that indeed, he had been successful in his responsibilities, and did not feel a need to engage his son on a more personal basis.

Paul stopped several feet from his patriarch and said in a quiet voice, "Father, may I speak to you for a few moments?" His father slowly looked up from his studies, nodding in agreement. As he looked directly into the boy's eyes, he realized again that the one thing that they physically had in common, was that they both had an unusual color of green in their eyes, as opposed to most of the people of their ethnic background having brown eyes.

Paul's thick, black wavy hair that curled at the ends against the lower back of his neck contrasted greatly with the thin white receding hair that he himself wore short. Also, he recognized that when Paul would reach full growth, he would be much taller than he was, in addition to his son having a broader frame and being more muscular. He observed these things, feeling no emotion inside of him. After all, was he not a man of intellect and not one of frivolous feelings?

Paul felt the same uncomfortable feeling as he now stood in front of his father as he did in almost all the occasions that they had conversations. Often times Paul would have his meals in the large kitchen with some of the servants, where he could enjoy a lively exchange of information, providing he carefully chose his subjects. He tried not to discuss things with them in which they had no knowledge. This contrasted greatly with those times when he ate with his father and mother in their large formal dining room, in which very few words were spoken.

"Father, in approximately two months I will be through with my studies. I am asking your permission that I would then be able to travel to the Holy Land, allowing me to further develop my education. If you are willing to grant me this request, and provide me

the funds to travel across the Great Sea, I promise I would then find work to support myself after I arrive. This would provide me an opportunity to have a greater understanding of our religion and our relationship with God, while at the same time I will learn the ways to become a responsible adult."

His father hesitated for a few moments, while he was allowing his thoughts to be collected, to be transferred into words. At first Paul thought that his request was going to be rejected, but then his father responded "I have also given thought for many months that your traveling to the Holy Land would be in your best interest. Your education has prepared you for possibilities of pursuing many different things, but was not intended that you become a common laborer."

His father continued to look deeply into Paul's eyes, carefully choosing his words. He wanted his son to realize his decision was indeed one that was based on logic and considerable thought and not on emotion or in trying to please his son's request without there being justification.

He continued "I will provide you with the funds that will allow you to find opportunities for yourself. You should learn how to manage your money and then allow your money to earn additional money. Once you are settled down in Jerusalem, you should try to purchase small retail stalls or shops. Try to purchase these by providing the owner a portion of the funds in advance, but the majority over as long a period as possible.

"In the meantime, you can rent out the facilities to others, whether it is making products, or providing services, or the selling of goods. You can charge them a monthly rent that would be greater than what you are paying monthly to the people that you have made the purchase from. As you accumulate more income from your monthly rent, you can then buy additional stalls, until you have many different sources working for you, providing you even greater income."

His father hesitated as he tried to evaluate Paul's response to his instructions. The young man appeared to be showing great respect to his suggestions, so he continued. "I want you to become self sufficient, learn how to manage your money, how to evaluate opportunities and how to negotiate the purchase as well as the renting of these facilities.

"Remember, if you work with good people you get good results. If you do business with people who are dishonest or incompetent, you will get bad results. You must learn how to evaluate people, how to analyze situations, how to negotiate in order to protect yourself and how to create benefits for yourself. Do You understand what I'm sharing with you?"

Paul hesitated, and took several steps forward so that he stood directly in front of his father. He suddenly knelt down on his knees, taking his father's hands in his, and looked into his eyes. "Father, I would never disappoint you. I am so grateful for your support. Thank you with all my heart".

His father turned his head away from Paul so his son couldn't see the tear that was beginning to roll down the side of his left cheek. Paul realized, in spite of his father trying to hide it, that he was embarrassed as well as moved by this conversation. Paul

immediately stood up, looking down at the ground, as he retreated several steps so his father would not know that he had recognized this rare moment of emotion from him. He continued to retreat back. Again, he whispered, loud enough for his father to hear, "Thank you father, thank you," and turned and left the library.

Chapter 3
The Surrounding

After declining breakfast from the wife of his landlord, Saul went back into the house, walking towards the hallway at the rear of the spacious kitchen. He then turned right, stepping quietly along the stone floor until he reached the wing of the house, which was the portion that he rented from his landlord. The only room that he used in common with the husband and wife was the kitchen, during the times when he joined them at a meal.

There was one large room that was his, which provided him a combination of functions. It included not only his bed, but also a soft divan and one window that were made out of a hazy glass, which was decorated with woven curtains. Beneath the window was a brazier, which Saul would use to burn firewood during the cold weather in order to provide heat and warmth to his quarters.

There were two tables, one next to the bed, and one in front of the

divan for reading or writing, in which both held large candlesticks to provide nighttime lighting. The floor of his quarters was also made of stone, but there were woven rugs scattered around the room in order to provide comfort to his feet rather than walking on the cold stone floor in the winter.

Behind this all-purpose room was a small room, which enabled him to perform his bathroom activities rather than having to go outside. There was a wooden ledge that was fastened to the rear wall, which had a round hole cut into it, as well as a partition in the front. The floor below the hole was of dirt, and had been graded in such a manner that it was lower as it went towards the outside wall.

A funnel like opening had been created where the floor of the house met the dirt, enabling the waste products to go out of the house into the ruts that had been created in the rear yard into a cistern type system. There was also a bucket of clean water sitting on the shelf next to the opening of the hole, allowing Saul to be able to pour out some of the water when he was through with his activities, creating a flushing system.

Since the water was clean, there was also a ladle with a curved end that was attached in a resting manner against the bucket, in order to be able to draw water to rinse out his mouth, after he had cleaned his teeth with a soft cloth using a paste made out of honey and an abrasive material.

Saul removed his nightgown that he had worn to bed. He began to select what he would wear for the day from the clothes hanging on numerous pegs on the wall to the left of his bed. Realizing that he would be walking along some very dusty roads from his house until he arrived at the marketplace, he chose a dark robe for his outdoor activities, as did most people in Jerusalem.

It was the custom that white tunics, or white cloaks, and other light colored items of wardrobe were generally confined to be worn indoors, or on special occasions, whereas dark garments were selected for the outdoor environment in order to camouflage the stains or dirt that they would be exposed to. The skirt of his garment ended slightly above his knees and his upper garment had wide sleeves that fell slightly below his elbows. He wanted to dress comfortably for he knew that it was going to be quite hot before the day was over.

On his feet he wore sandals, which had crisscross straps of leather going half way up his calves. Under his skirt there was a belt made of rope in which a money pouch with holes through it was fastened to the rope, and contained copper coins as well as shekels.

Saul ran a wire brush through his hair as he inspected himself in front of a very fuzzy mirror made of slightly darkened glass. He smiled at himself with approval, and felt a feeling of pride pass through him, aware that he was a striking figure. His skin was tanned, which made an attractive background to his green eyes and large white teeth, which flashed when he smiled.

Saul was committed, not only to wanting to maintain his good looks so that he would be attractive to the young women that were available in great abundance throughout Jerusalem, but also towards his cleanliness. He tried to bathe at least once every other day in the large copper tub that was located in the room that was designed for his bathroom activities. He would draw buckets of water from the

well behind the house and heat the water in the bathtub with a brazier.

As Saul began his descent down the streets leading from the hillside house to the market place, he walked very carefully to be sure that he did not step in any animal feces. He turned to his right so that he could walk through the neighborhood that he most enjoyed, looking beyond the gates and fences of the villas that he passed.

Some properties had high stone block walls and iron gates. In front of the walls were fragrant white flowers and jasmine trees. He particularly enjoyed the fragrance of the lilacs, as well as the climbing evergreen shrubs against the stone walls located between the spacing of myrtle trees and palm trees.

It would take him approximately twenty-five minutes to get from his house to the market place located in the center of the city. As he descended further down the hill, the houses became smaller. Eventually the neighborhood dramatically changed. The houses were either attached to one another, or so close together that only one person at a time could walk between them.

In these less expensive neighborhoods, the roofs of the houses were flat, and one could walk from one rooftop to another. At night time, during the hot and uncomfortable weather, the people would sit on their rooftops on chairs, and have conversations with their neighbors, waiting for the night air to cool them down, before they retired to their beds.

Saul was very conscious of the narrow windows absent of any glass that had been designed within these smaller houses. The windows were too small for a robber to be able to crawl through, but yet allowed some circulation of air, as well as allowing the smoke from the braziers during the winter time to escape out of the house. Saul observed all these things with his eyes without having to give any thought to them. Instead, he was thinking of his schedule for this day.

First he would visit two of the three shops that he owned to make sure things were in order, and that his renters were attending to them properly. He would then have a late morning breakfast with some of his friends. But his most favorite time of the day would occur when he joined other men along the steps of the portico of the Great Temple for the exciting and informative discussions that they had almost on a daily basis.

It was here during these meetings, as they sat on the wide low steps of the temple built by Herod, relaxing in the shade away from the hot sun or on the other side of the temple during the cooler weather so they could enjoy the sunshine. It was here that Saul felt alive as he absorbed the greater lessons of life. It was during these discussions that they were solving the problems not only in Jerusalem, but also in other parts of Israel, as well as the Roman Empire.

How were they functioning under Roman occupation? What could they do, without alienating the Romans, to improve their way of life? Would there ever come a day that the Romans would no longer occupy their land, and under what conditions could that possibly happen?

But Saul had his greatest enjoyment during the discussions regarding religion. What is our relationship with God? Does God

intervene in our lives, and if so in what way? What is the purpose of life? What is their understanding of what happens after death in comparing the belief of the Pharisees as opposed to the belief of the Saducees? Saul loved the heated debates over what parts of the Bible should be taken literally, and what parts were meant to try and create a point as opposed to have actually happened. Saul always attended these discussions with a sense of excitement and anticipation.

What a great experience, thought Saul, to be able to sit on the beautiful steps of the Great Temple, sheltered from the sun by the majestic, imposing white marble structure of the walls of the temple on a hot summer day; to sit amidst of this learned group made up of intellectuals, pessimists, optimists, praisers and criticizers and people from many different walks of life. What a glorious day and what a glorious opportunity. Thank you Jerusalem, for these wonderful experiences.

Chapter 4
The Farewell

Paul would always have fond memories of his farewell from Tarsus. The evening before his departure, his tutors joined together in presenting a light hearted and affectionate dinner party including an abundance of wine. This moving event took place on large wooden tables outdoors in the garden that was shaded by the carob and sycamore trees.

A short distance away, swans and birds lazily sat on the edges of a small pond. Large plates of steaming food were served including boiled lamb and spicy meats wrapped in leaves, along with artichokes, stewed beans, cabbages, bread, cheese, figs and grapes. For dessert the tutors and Saul were served almonds, honey sweetened dates and pastries.

Mordecai, his tutor of Jewish learning, suggested to Paul, "My

dear, wonderful student, may I offer you a thought? Here in Tarsus, you are a Roman citizen, Paulus, from the house of Zerah. But in the Holy Land, it is important they know you as a Jew and one who is of Pharisee beliefs. I suggest while in the Holy Land, that you use your Hebrew name of Saul, rather than Paulus. Then, you will not draw the suspicions of your fellow Jews."

Then Demis, his Greek tutor of philosophy stated, "And remember Paul, in Jerusalem they identify you by the name of your father, or where you were from. If you are from Jerusalem, and people know your father, then they will address you as Saul, the son of Abraham or Saul, the son of Simon. But if people don't know your father, because you are from another part of the world, they will then call you, Saul of Macedonia, or Saul of Damascus. In your case, since they don't know your father's name is Zerah, they will refer to you as Saul of Tarsus."

Demis continued, as he raised his goblet of wine in a salute. "So Saul of Tarsus, make us proud. Carry yourself with pride and dignity, for you represent all of us who have spent years making you the wise young man that you are, filling your head with the knowledge of the world and with the philosophy of the great minds of the past. When you speak, you speak for all of us."

"And yes," Demis shouted with a playful gesture towards his fellow tutors. "And when you make love with the young women, you make love for all of us," and they all laughed and raised their goblets and drank in agreement.

Paul felt a great tenderness in his heart. He had not realized how much he loved these men who had spent years teaching him with great patience and tenacity, these men of great learning and wisdom. Paul was positive that he would always be consciously aware that his education was a gift that was given to him by his father and delivered by these wonderful men of learning.

Paul then stood up before them, and held his goblet in front of him at arm's length, and with a great amount of affection and sincerity, stated, "You shall always be in my thoughts, as well as in my prayers. Whether I'm discussing philosophy or the laws of God, I shall always be speaking for you. For I shall always remember with gratitude, your teachings and your words of wisdom. And may I remain also in your thoughts and your prayers?"

The following morning, Paul stood on the road that passed through his father's property that traveled eastward towards the Great Sea. His personal belongings had been tied to saddlebags on his favorite donkey. He would be traveling the seven miles to the sea along with a servant as his protector, whose name was Tola.

Together they would arrive at the mouth of the Cyndus River, where it meets the Great Sea, in order for Paul to begin his journey. Then Tola would return home with the two donkeys and Paul would be on his own for the first time to begin the first day of his new life.

Paul's farewell to his parents was very brief. There was a feeling that Paul as well as his father and mother wanted to express words of tenderness to one another but didn't know how to do so. His mother stood very quietly with a sad grim look on her face, her eyes filled with a look of anxiety as they said goodbye. She embraced Paul and pressed her cheek against him for a moment and then pulled back as if she was embarrassed, as she glanced over to her husband.

Zerah then grasped Paul with his right hand around Paul's right upper arm, in which Paul's right hand pressed around his father's upper arm, in the traditional handshake that was used by the Romans. They stood in this position for a number of seconds, both staring at each other's eyes without saying any words. It was their way of saying good-bye to one another.

They both knew there was a hidden love and respect, which couldn't be expressed in words, but both understood. The thought briefly crossed Paul's mind that this may indeed be the last time that he would see his father, considering his age and health.

Later in the day Paul found himself looking over the railing of the merchant ship as it was pulling away from the land of Celicia that he wouldn't see again for many years. There were people of many different nationalities on the ship, both men and women, who were also traveling to the Holy Land, most for reasons of business. Paul felt very confident among them as he introduced himself and shared small talk. At eighteen years old, he had almost reached his full height, although not yet totally filled out as far as his physical form. He was slightly taller than the average man, and his tan skin and green eyes with his thick black wavy hair was looked upon appreciatively by the female passengers.

He was careful to make it appear that these looks went unnoticed, so he didn't bring discomfort to their husbands or male companions and he made an effort to treat every person with the same respect regardless of their appearance or apparent shortcomings. He thought to himself, that if he were smarter or more educated than his fellow passengers, it was best that he kept that to himself.

He had been taught that you don't make friends by making others feel inferior. He didn't participate in their games of gambling during the voyage, for not only did he not want to take the risk of losing his own money, but also he had no desire to win the money of others. He spent his hours on the ship going from one group to another enjoying the quiet discussions, and learning from each person, as he questioned them about their past and their ambitions of the future. This was his way of learning more and more about life. His inquisitive mind was like a sponge that was never saturated.

The ship arrived at its destination, which was the seaport city of Caesarea, on the western shores of the Great Sea, in the province of Samaria, in the land of Israel. Saul stood on the deck overlooking the wharf in the early morning air, mesmerized with the incredible sights before him as the ship slowly moved into port. There was activity all around, people selling and trading and others making themselves available for hire, who would be paid to transfer goods from the docks to locations within the city.

Some of them had carts with long wooden handles attached to platforms, in which the goods would sit upon, which were moved by two large wheels and the weight of the manpower that pushed it. There were no animals located at the port, because it was too noisy and crowded, which would cause a distraction and frighten the animals. Saul couldn't contain his excitement as he watched this incredible scene unfold before his eyes, many people of different colors, shouts and yells of obscenities in different languages, and the chaos and confusion of a busy seaport.

That afternoon Saul found a family to provide him room and

board. He would spend his days wandering around the city finding new excitement and new adventures on a daily basis. Some times he would engage into group discussions with six or seven other people. Even though he was inclined to wear clothes that were more expensive and of higher quality than the local people, he tried to dress in their same fashion so he wouldn't look and feel out of place.

By the time that three and a half months had gone by, Paul had lost any sign of shyness that he may have brought within him to Caesarea and this new world. He now felt confident and at ease in this new environment, as well in his discussions among his new acquaintances. It was now time to move on. Paul made plans to take a ship to the next port city of Joppa, which was south of Caesarea. The trip wasn't very long and it was uneventful. From Joppa, he then traveled due west to the magnificent city of Jerusalem, and the new world and new life that was waiting for him.

Chapter 5
Dining with friends

Upon arriving at the marketplace, Saul immediately went to the stall that was the location of one of his renters. It was a stall that was rented by a Syrian family now living in Jerusalem. They were the seller of tents that were weaved and made in Damascus by their relatives. The tent was closed on three sides, with another part of the tent material laid horizontally, forming a roof in order to provide shade during the hot weather.

Saul paid his respects, first hoping that they were all in good health, before discussing their business activities. In addition to a fixed fee that they paid Saul monthly, they also paid him a percentage of the income that they received from the sale or rental of their tents. This way, it eased their burden during times when sales were slow, and it increased both their income as well as Saul's,

during the busiest seasons.

But at all times Saul's fixed rent that he received, regardless of how the sales and rentals were doing, enabled him to pay the monthly amount to the original people who sold him the stall. With the purchase of the stall from the original seller, Saul not only inherited the tent makers, who were now his customers, but also the location of the stall and its equipment.

Following his visit, Saul then went to the second stall that he owned, in which his renters were selling products, such as cosmetics, embroideries, shawls, brushes and other related items. This stall was rented and operated by two sisters, who had built up their clientele over many years. Most of their goods were received by companies who acted as wholesalers of imported goods from traders who brought in their products from other countries, and then were made available to the retailers, such as the two sisters. Saul enjoyed his relationship with both of his renters whom he believed to be honest hard working people and there was a mutual respect by both the renters as well as the landlord.

The time was now late in the morning and the activity in the marketplace was very brisk. Most of the people were trying to complete their shopping in the morning in order to escape the time of the day when it would become uncomfortable from the hot weather during the afternoon.

Saul then walked through the retail stalls to another part of the marketplace, which housed the many different eating establishments. He soon came across an area in which wooden chairs and tables were located servicing several different eating establishments. As

Saul approached this area, he found two of his friends already seated sipping from their wine goblets with a pitcher of spiced wine on the table.

"Aha, our good friend from Tarsus, so you have found us," spoke a very large young man with a bushy beard and pleasant smile on his round wide face. "Yes," Saul responded, "How could I miss you? You take up two seats, and your voice can be heard all the way to the Wailing Wall." The three men laughed together, as Saul took a seat across from his large friend Aaron and to the left of his other friend, a thin man dressed in a dark gray tunic of soft linen, whose name was Talah. Talah wore rings on his fingers, a bracelet on each wrist and a necklace. He was beardless, as was Saul and his thin narrow face was in sharp contrast with that of the burly companion who was dressed in a simple robe of course cloth.

"Saul, you must taste the fruitcake. You will swear that it must have been made by your grandmother," commented Talah. Saul responded, "I'm sure that it will. In fact, perhaps she is working back in the kitchen, which would explain her disappearance twenty years ago." Again, they all laughed together. Saul motioned the young lady over, who was waiting on the tables. "I see my friends have already begun to eat, so I will try to catch up with them." Saul proceeded in ordering some broiled fish along with hard crusted bread, aged goat cheese and an assortment of ripe local fruits, and poured himself a goblet of scented wine from the pitcher.

The three young men began to have a discussion of the events surrounding their daily lives. Aaron spoke in his loud, booming voice, with great excitement, about a wrestling match that he had

recently witnessed at the arena, describing in detail the accomplishment of one of his favorite athletes. Talah spoke of a young lady that he had been pursuing, whose father didn't approve of his efforts. "You would think I was trying to marry her, rather than just trying to bed her. I don't want to be his son in law any more than he wants to be my father in law," Talah complained.

"Maybe it's the other way around" Saul responded. "Maybe he would prefer that you did marry her, rather than your trying to win her heart and body." "Huh, I hadn't thought about that," responded Talah, who had a terrible reputation for being a womanizer. "And you Saul," asked Aaron, "Have you found the lucky woman yet who will someday bear your children?" Saul responded "You can't find what you are not looking for, Aaron."

The men continued with their causal conversation, sometimes making fun of each other or themselves as they enjoyed their light meal. They paid the young lady that was waiting on them for their meals and began to say their good-byes as they rose from their chairs. Saul told them that he was now on his way over to the Great Temple in order to participate in some discussions and invited Aaron to join him. Aaron declined, and the three men embraced each other and then went their separate ways.

Saul intentionally took the longer route on the way to the temple heading in a westerly direction through the bazaar. He passed women with baskets on their heads, musicians sitting cross-legged on the dirt in the shade playing their instruments, and an occasional small crowd of people surrounding a comedian in one location and an orator in another.

Saul loved walking through the bazaar, listening to the sounds of the people bargaining or yelling out their wares, as well as enjoying the different smells from the bakeries and wine shops, and the children shouting at each other as they played games while their parents shopped in the various stalls. Jerusalem indeed, was an exciting world to live in.

Chapter 6
Temple talk

Saul eventually reached the Great Temple. He always felt a sense of astonishment, because of its size and its magnificence. Approximately six hundred years earlier, the original temple as well as the City of Jerusalem had been destroyed, when the Jews were defeated and taken in captivity to Babylon. The only portion of the original temple built by Solomon that still existed was the Inner Sanctum, which contained the Holy of the Holy's.

King Herod was now building a new temple, including magnificent courts, stone pillars sixty feet in height, double colonnades of stone that were fifty feet long and arched entry pillars that were forty feet high. Although the construction of the main temple had been completed by Herod's workmen within an eighteen-month period approximately forty years earlier, there were other

portions of the temple that were still under construction.

The temple had exits and entrances to various courts, with a total of nine gates. It also included an outer court for women who were not allowed to get any closer to the actual sanctuary, other than within that court. Saul passed through the outer court, through the gates of the inner court and began to circle to his left. He knew that the group would be sitting on the steps of the portico on the north side of the temple in order to be able to be in the shade as opposed to sitting in the sunshine on the south side of the temple.

As Saul approached the steps, he saw that there were seven men already seated, forming a semicircle, in which four of the men were sitting on the seventh step up from the ground, and two were seated on the fifth and sixth step to their left and another man sat on their opposite side on the sixth step. Saul crossed in front of the group, to sit on the step below the man who was seated on step six. Saul recognized five of the men as regulars of the group who usually met five days a week, with the exception of Friday and Saturday, the day of Sabbath.

One of the men called out "Ah, and here is Saul, one of our brighter participants. He knows when to talk, and when to be silent. Saul, say hello to Eleazar, the son of Hamul, and also to Jamin of Tiberias. Men, may I introduce you to Saul of Tarsus, if not the oldest of our group, certainly the most handsome." Saul smiled at the group, and nodded his head at the two new men.

With the exception of one of the men sitting across from Saul who was approximately the same age as he, the other men were either slightly or much older then Saul. Four of the men were dressed in various outfits including lightweight cloth tunics, but three of them were dressed more like Saul, wearing a skirt that stopped above the knees, and a pullover cloth jersey that was short sleeved.

The men dressed similar to Saul were generally younger men who were in better physical condition and, as it was the custom, the older men as well as those who were not in good physical condition were more inclined to wear tunics, robes or cloaks. One of the older men turned to the newcomers, and stated "Perhaps we should hear from Saul, as to his opinion regarding his beliefs of what happens to us following death. Saul is not only a Pharisee but he has also been taught by some very learned rabbis from his part of the world when he was younger."

Saul looked at the man, and asked, "What were you discussing?" The man answered "Well, we were talking about the difference in the belief of life after death, between the Pharisees and the Sadducees." As he motioned to a man on his left, he stated, "Hamul was explaining what he believed was the position of Sadducees, and why it differs from the Pharisees. Go ahead Hamul, and explain it again."

Hamul began "Well, unlike the Pharisees, the Sadducees, do not claim that we have knowledge of what happens after death. Has any man ever returned from death? It is one thing to teach certain things, and it is another to experience them. Since we are not able to share our experience as to what happens after death, then we must acknowledge that we don't know. Only God knows. And that is why we take the position that we don't know what happens after death. I

am positive that I am more certain than you, that I do not know what happens at death, then you can by telling me that you do know what happens after death."

Saul hesitated for a moment and gathered his thoughts before he answered. He then said "The fact that you are positive that you don't know, only assures us of one thing, and that is that you don't know. It doesn't provide us evidence of what happens, but only instead, your acknowledgment of your limited knowledge," Saul retorted. "But in reality, there is truth to be found, either through logic, or through experience. We Pharisees do indeed believe that after we die, our spirits are eventually born again to new children, so that we continue to experience the cycle of life, as well as the cycle of death."

One of the other men commented "That is a good argument Saul. Because you, Hamul, as a Sadducee may not know the answer, that doesn't mean there is no answer. Go ahead Saul, continue."

Saul looked down at the stairs below him, as if in deep thought. It was not so much that Saul was making an evaluation, but instead he was allowing his mind to function in carefully choosing the words to express himself.

"The fact that you believe something different than me doesn't mean that you will not experience the same as I will. There is no question that we all believe in our God, the God of Israel and the God of all men. What purpose does it serve that a child could lose his life, and that child would have died and no longer exist? But you're not saying he won't exist, but only that you don't know the answer. So, I will share with you that which is my understanding."

Saul continued, "Just as life must have a purpose, so must death. Death is a transition from that which is our life as we know it, into a different realm, in which our spirit continues to exist. This means that we continue to have our intellect, our personality and our memories." One of the older men shouted "You mean I must have this personality forever. Why can't I trade it in for a new one when I die?" But another one of their companions retorted "Why wait until you die? Why can't we have you change it now, so we can all enjoy you more?" And they all roared.

Saul answered "But you can do both. Certainly you can change your personality now, if you choose, but even with more certainty when you have the wisdom of your spirit mind, when you have been separated from your body in death, then you shall truly know what is worth retaining and what is worth changing. It's while you are studying and learning about yourself after death, it's then that you recognize what is truth as opposed to what is false. And I was taught that once you have discovered truth, and have acquired knowledge of how you must amend for the things that you did wrong in your lifetime, it's only then that you're allowed to proceed in returning back to earth; for you shall then be born into a new lifetime, in which your soul shall have a fresh start, so that you may practice that which you have previously learned and correct for that which you have done wrong, in order to make amends."

Again, the man that first introduced Saul to the newcomers stated "And that is why we should not be judgmental of God regarding the loss of life of a child. We Pharisees know that the child shall be born again, and be given another opportunity to improve upon his new life

and to make amends for sins and wrong doings from his previous lifetimes."

The debate continued between the Pharisees and the Sadducees, each arguing that their belief system was correct. At times, the speakers chose to use logic, other times humor, and sometimes they became quite agitated and spoke their positions with a great deal of passion and intensity. Finally, the man that had been introduced to Saul as Jamin of Tiberias spoke up; "There is a man that I would like to introduce you to, who will be in Jerusalem tomorrow. His name is Jeshua, although the Greeks call him Jesus. He is a man of tremendous wisdom. If I can persuade him to join us here tomorrow, I feel he could enlighten us on many of these Issues. May I bring him?"

"What is his father's name? I know several men by the name of Jeshua," one of the men asked. Jamin responded, "I don't know his father's name, for he's not from Jerusalem. He is from Capernaum, but he's known as Jeshua of Nazareth, because his parents originally lived in Nazareth when he was born. But he's an extraordinary individual. I have only heard him speak once, but I know that you will be impressed."

Individuals from the group responded by saying "Bring him" and "let him come. We would love to hear what he has to say." And another complained, "Capernaum is known for its fishermen, not for its scholars, but bring him anyway. We shall look forward to meeting him."

The discussions then turned to other controversial subjects, some related to religious beliefs and others dealing with contemporary issues in Jerusalem. Several hours had gone by, and the shadows from the magnificent temple were now falling deeper across the stairs onto the portico as the sun moved across the sky further into the west. The group now began to break up and say their good-byes.

Saul headed towards the gates, exiting out of the same entrances that he entered and decided to stroll once again through the bazaar and the marketplace before he began his journey up the hillside to his home. He thought of his visit with his two friends at lunchtime, and the contrast between them. He actually enjoyed the company of his burly friend Aaron more than he did of Talah.

Aaron had a great sense of humor, and was a very stable person, married with two young children. He had a great enjoyment of life, and very few things bothered him. On the other band, Talah was a very tense individual, who seemed constantly to be creating one crisis after another in his life. As soon as be thought he solved one, he created another and never seemed to be satisfied. Saul thought, perhaps it was the diversity of the two individuals, which attracted them to him. It's the difference in people that make this life interesting, Saul mused.

His thoughts then transferred to the heated discussions that he recently participated in on the stairs of the Great Temple. Saul thought to himself, "What could be more important than having a positive belief system in what happens after death? If you were to die, and believed you no longer existed after death, then what is the purpose of life?"

As a Pharisee, he did have an absolute belief in life after death, and that we are born again at some future time after death, in order

to receive the awards of our past lives or to be punished for our failures, until we receive redemption. But, he thought, that indeed, if the Pharisees were wrong and the Sadducees were right, and there was no life after death, what impact would that have had on his present life? Would he have the same values? Would he live his life exactly the same in trying to distinguish right from wrong? And is our only experience confined to the fifty or sixty years that we live on this earth and there was no such thing as a reward system or retribution?

His thoughts then turned to the new man that his group would be meeting with tomorrow, the one from Capernaum. If he was as enlightened and as brilliant as the man from Tiberias had said, perhaps he will have some new insight to some of these mysteries of life. Yes, tomorrow should be an interesting day.

As many hundreds of years passed into the future, most people of both the Jewish faith as well as the Christian faith would lose the knowledge that during the time of Jeshua, 2,000 years ago, the majority of the people of the Jewish faith in the Holy Land did believe in reincarnation. The population of Pharisees was greater then that of Sadducees, so the majority of the Jews within the Holy Land embraced the belief of transformation of the soul, reincarnation.

In the 17th century Rabbi Manasseb ben Israel wrote " The belief of the doctrine of the transmigration of souls, reincarnation, is a firm and infallible dogma accepted by the whole assemblage of our religion with one accord, so that there is none to be found who would dare to deny it. Indeed, there is a great number of sages in

Israel who hold firm to this doctrine so that they made it into a dogma, a fundamental point of our religion. We are therefore in duty bound to obey and accept this dogma with acclimation."

During the 20th century we find that the Judaic religion has been separated into mainly three groups identified as orthodox, conservative, reform, and those who are Hasidic Jews. Those three main groups, excluding Hasidism, are carry forwards of those who were Sadducees 2,000 years ago, in that they primarily take the position that we do not know what happens to the soul after death, for only God knows. But the Hasidic Jews, although being a very small minority of Judaism, do indeed continue to embrace reincarnation. It is found in the Universal Jewish Encyclopedia the following quote "The doctrines of transmigration of souls, appears often in the Kabala; it is found in organized form in the Zohhar, and in Hasidism it becomes a universal belief. The soul has no sex, which is determined by the body and may vary from incarnation to incarnation."

This information is important for those of you readers who may have assumed that the author has taken the liberty of creating religious beliefs of the Jews who lived 2,000 years ago, including those of Paul and Jesus, which were not consistent with the truth. It is just the opposite, that modern religious teachers of both Christianity and Judaism are either not aware of what indeed is truth, or have chosen to ignore the truth, most likely the former.

Chapter 7
Dinner Talk

That evening Saul ate a very light meal at home, which he enjoyed, at the kitchen table with his landlord Kohath and his wife Jocelyn. "Saul, you seem so quiet this evening. Why are you so deep in thought?" Saul was very fond of his outgoing landlord as well as his wife. Kohath was a man of intelligence but had simple beliefs.

He was a person who didn't believe in making things complicated and tried to avoid confrontations or difficulties. He was a wine merchant, who enjoyed his work, but also didn't consume wine himself. He had developed respect and admiration for Saul over the last three years that Saul had lived with his family. "Why am I so deep in thought?" asked Saul, repeating Kohath's question. "I'm not sure, but I have the sense that something very important is going to

happen to me tomorrow."

"I don't want to invade your privacy, but are you comfortable telling us what this is about?" asked Kohath. Saul hesitated, and then answered, "I can't. I'm really not sure. It's just a feeling I have." Saul continued, "Have you ever heard of a man named Jeshua who is from Capernaum, but is known as Jeshua of Nazareth?"

"No, I haven't. I know very few people from Capernaum. Very few people from the province of Galilee travel this way to the province of Judea, since their province is not occupied by the Romans. I think they're uncomfortable when they come here and see all the soldiers," Kohath answered.

Jocelyn quietly ate her meal as she listened to the conversation between the men. She then spoke out saying "Also as you may know Saul, the Jews in the province of Galilee are quite different than the Jews in the province of Judea. Because of the wars and occupation by other countries over the years in their region, many of them are like me, in that some of their fore bearers were not Jews. Some of the Jews married non-Jews, so they are not as religious as the Jews in Judea."

Saul responded, "That's true. In fact, some of the Jews in the provinces of Sumaria and Galilee don't practice religion at all. They are neither Pharisees, Sadducees nor Essenes."

Jocelyn looked at Saul slightly puzzled and asked, "How is that possible? How are they Jews and not practice their religion?" Saul then answered Jocelyn, "It's no different than it is in your country. Can you not be a Persian yet not practice the religious beliefs of the Persians?"

Kohath leaned back in his chair and started laughing. "And what religion is it that the Persians practice? You mean praying to a lemon tree?" All three of them laughed together. Kohath continued, "Who is the man Jeshua that you ask about?"

"I'm not sure," Saul answered. "I just have the strangest feeling inside of me. But I shall find out tomorrow. But tonight," Saul raised his voice in glee with a smile on his face, letting them know he was changing the subject. "Tonight, I shall spend in the arms of my beautiful friend Leah." And Saul began quietly to sing the words of a Hebrew love song telling of a man and his loved one dancing and kissing in the dark.

Jocelyn turned to her husband and said "And you, why don't you sing love songs about me?" Kohath responded "I do, every night, in my dreams." The three dining companions laughed in appreciation of Kohath's humor and the warm feelings they had towards each other.

Saul left the house in early evening as the night sky was approaching with its veils of darkness and secrecy. He walked in a southeasterly direction through a neighborhood, about half way down the hillside, until he came to a park that was wooded and had a beautiful view overlooking the city below. He then walked to a grove of sycamore trees, and found Leah resting on a blanket under a tree. To her far side was a basket containing cheese, grapes and a container of wine.

"Oh, you spoil me, how can I live without you?" Saul jokingly asked. Leah turned her face to Saul, her large soulful eyes looking into Saul's. "I hope you shall find you are not able to. Then I shall

own you and make you my slave," she answered as Saul lowered himself beside her. He took her into his arms and slowly brought her against him, feeling the feminism of her body pressed against his chest and his loins. Their lips soon found each other and they shared a soft but intimate kiss that lasted a long time, neither wanting to bring the pleasure of that intimacy to an end.

They sat for three hours under the branches of the Sycamore trees, sometimes snacking on the cheese and grapes, sometimes sipping wine from the two goblets Leah had brought in her basket, sometimes enjoying the frivolous and sweet words that filled their conversation and sometimes pausing for their lips to meet, each kiss becoming more passionate and more intense.

The bottom of the heavens above now lit up with hundreds of stars that shown on the plate that separated heaven from the earth. Occasionally they would see a star fall from the plate and shoot across the sky. The moon was two thirds full, so Saul could make out the features of his lovely companion.

Leah had black hair that she wore slightly above her shoulders. Her skin was a light brown, tanned by the sun. She had high cheekbones, a gentle rounded chin and a smile that could melt a robber's heart. Saul knew he loved her, and although he had other female friends, none could make his heart beat as fiercely as could Leah. This was both a blessing as well as a punishment, for he did not want to feel dependent on her for his happiness.

Many times when Leah brought up their relationship and wanted to know of their future, Saul had been candid and told her of his dilemma. He loved her, but didn't want to consider a marriage contract. As painful as it was, he encouraged her to see other men. Leah now turned to Saul with a very serious look on her face. "Let's forget you and me for the moment. But don't you some day want to have children of your own, and a family to care for and to share your love with?"

"I don't know how to answer your question Leah." Leah interrupted before Saul could continue, "But why not just answer it honestly? I truly need to know your thoughts". Saul hesitated; searching within his own mind for the answer to what was indeed an honest and forthright question.

The answer was not one that he spent a lot of time thinking about in the past, but he knew in the subconscious level of his mind, that indeed he must have some conclusive thoughts regarding how he felt about his own future, even though he had never expressed them before, or tried to verbalize them.

He answered her, "I feel there is something very important that I must do with my life. I don't envision myself living in a house on a hillside with several children, visiting my renters each day at the market place, and giving my money to the moneylenders to give to others so that I can make more money. Leah, even though I can't answer you specifically, I feel that there are greater things in life that are demanded of me, and until I understand what they are, and have experienced them, I don't want to make a decision in my life that will require me to go in a different direction. I say this to you, even though I don't know the direction that I'm talking about. Does any of this make any sense to you?"

"Not really," Leah answered. She looked at Saul with a very

gentle look, a slight, loving smile on her face, realizing that he was speaking from the heart, and that this was painful for him. She didn't question his love, but she didn't understand his reluctance in having them commit themselves to each other and to live their lives together.

There really was nothing more to say at this moment. They both proceeded in tasting the wine and enjoying the cheese and grapes that Leah had brought in her basket, and remained silent for the next few minutes, looking at the sky; sometimes looking below at the lights of the city created from the burning oil lamps and lit candles in the windows.

Even though neither of them expressed it, they were both thinking the same thoughts. Would Leah someday find another man to be her husband and accept the fact that the man she truly loved was unable to make a commitment. Saul realized there would come a day that would be tremendously painful in his life, if and when she did make that decision.

However, he would try to understand and recognize that he alone was the one responsible for his pain and therefore he must suffer without complaint. And Leah, she did not intend to the live the rest of her life alone. She knew that within her womb, some day children would be conceived, which she would care for and nourish, and hopefully the love for her children would compensate for the love that she would not be able to share with Saul, as husband and wife.

As the night wore on, as one by one the lights in the city below were extinguished. Later, Saul walked Leah to her home and then began his journey back to his rented house, in a westerly direction, higher up the hillside. Although he felt a sense of accomplished pleasure and physically relaxed, his soul and his heart pulsated in anticipation, for somehow deep in his being he had a distinct feeling that tomorrow was going to be a special day in his life.

Chapter 8
The Man from Galilee

When Saul appeared on the north side of the Great Temple portico the following day, nine of the men who normally met for their daily discussions were already there. Saul noticed that Jamin of Tiberias and his guest had not yet arrived. The group sat on the steps in the shade, chatting casually, not wanting to begin one of their heated debates until the new arrival had joined them. Only a short time had passed when four men turned the corner, approaching them, led by Jamin.

Saul's eyes immediately fell upon the man walking on the right hand side next to Jamin. He was tall and wore a gray tunic that stopped just above his sandals, which were made of medium brown leather, strapless, but with a thong across the toes. When he got closer, Saul noticed that his hands had been tanned by the sun, and

his fingers were delicate looking, yet oddly enough, appeared to be strong at the same time. The other two men with him were walking slightly behind the man from Galilee, looking somewhat awkward in comparison to the graceful, long strides and regal posture of the Galilean. *Jeshua*

While some of the men remained seated, Saul and several others stood up out of respect, to greet the newcomers. Saul walked down four steps so he was at the same level as Jamin and the new visitor, only an arm's length away. Standing close to them, Saul now realized that Jeshua was not as tall as he first appeared; yet he was still slightly taller than Saul.

He now looked at the man's face and was stunned. He was the most handsome man that Saul had ever seen. Like many people who had spent considerable time outdoors, his skin had been browned by the sun and his long, thick brown hair had streaks of gold and reddish highlights that had been caused by the sun. He had high cheekbones and full lips and his hair and beard were well groomed.

When Saul looked in his eyes, he was totally taken back. They were a very deep bluish gray, almost as if they were three dimensional, with large white pupils. "His eyes," thought Saul, "They are looking into my being. His eyes are touching my soul." Saul recaptured his normal composure and realized Jeshua had a slight smile on his lips as he was studying Saul in a gentle, loving way. The look in his eyes was not judgmental, yet Saul felt as if his entire being had been laid naked during the few moments that their eyes had met.

As Jamin was announcing to the group, "My friends, may I

introduce you to Jeshua of Nazareth," Jeshua reached out and placed his left hand on the right shoulder of Saul and said very softly, "Saul, son of Zerah, may God bless you." Saul smiled at Jeshua, taking a short step backwards, and then turned back to take his seat on the fourth step of the portico.

His voice shouted silently in his head, "How did he know my name and that my father's name was Zerah?" Saul was filled with many emotions, as he sat and fixed his gaze on the man from Capernaum, who now stood on the large slab of marble in front of the steps and the others all sat in a semi-circle slightly above him.

Jeshua then glanced at this two companions, then at the group, and said, "My two friends are Cephus and Andrew and they are brothers and fishermen from Bethsaida. You may also call Cephus, Peter, if you choose." The two men nodded to the group and began to climb the stairs, seating themselves behind and to the left of the listeners. Saul noted that Andrew was thinner and shorter than his brother, and had a gentle, nondescript, beardless face. His brother Peter was larger and huskier of build, had a thick, shaggy beard and carried the appearance of strength both in his body and his face.

Now they were all seated, except Jeshua, who quietly looked at the group, as if waiting for someone to begin the discussion. There was complete silence for many moments, but it was not uncomfortable. There was an aura of peace and serenity surrounding them as if Jeshua had intoxicated them all with his presence. Finally, one of the regulars asked, "You have come a long way. Did you just arrive today?"

"No, we arrived in Judea two days ago, and we have been staying

with friends who live in Bethany," Jeshua answered. "Oh," the man continued. "I have many friends in Bethany. Who were you staying with?" Jeshua responded, "There is a family in Bethany that I am very close to who are Magdalenes. I knew them from when they used to live in Magdala, which as you know, is not that far from Capernaum.

"The head of the household is Lazarus, and there are three sisters, one that has married and moved to Jericho with her husband, and the other two Mary and Martha, who live with their brother Lazarus." Another man in the group then spoke up, "Your friend Jamin from Tiberius speaks very highly of you. Are you a rabbi?"

"Aren't we all rabbis as well as pupils? The Lord does not reserve knowledge to just those that have been ordained, and neither does he prevent rabbis from learning from his disciples. If you have questions you wish to ask me, I'm willing to share my thoughts," Jeshua responded.

After a few seconds of silence, one of the men spoke up and then asked, "Jeshua, how does one account for joy and happiness in life? Why does God select that one shall be the master and one shall be the servant or the slave?"

Jeshua answered, in a gentle loving voice, "You are assuming that happiness shall come to the master and unhappiness to the servant or the slave. But this is not necessarily so. Happiness is found within. It has nothing to do with their position. There are many things that people seek to bring them happiness that instead they find that the pursuit of happiness, or even after having achieved that which they seek, does not bring them happiness, but instead, sadness. Happiness doesn't come from the possession of material things, nor does it come from a person's position in life. It comes from the love you share with your brothers and sisters, and your relationship with God."

One of the listeners then asked, in a quiet and respectful voice, "You say the love you share with your brothers and sisters. Do you mean family? What if you were an only child?"

Jeshua smiled gently at the question. Saul noticed his smile radiated, and his lips parted slightly, showing even, white teeth and his eyes and voice were mesmerizing. "Is it not so that God is our father and our mother? And yes, we are all the children of God? And if we are all the children of the same parent, are we not all brothers and sisters?"

Heads were nodding in agreement and then another voice asked, "Tell us Jeshua about death. What happens to a soul after death? Is there a continuous life, or do we no longer exist?" Jeshua again first looked directly at the questioner, and then at the audience as a whole, so they each felt as if they were being answered personally. "Your life is given to you by your spirit, which is a part of God. Yes, your spirit is part of God and that part of God resides within you. Your spirit is everlasting and immortal, for you are part of the oneness that is God."

Jeshua hesitated, allowing time for his words to be absorbed and then be continued, "Your body is a temple of God, and when it can no longer be of use, death is the doorway that spirit and soul exit from to continue its journey, but your spirit never dies." Saul was taken aback by the words. He never heard death explained in this

manner. There would be much to think about. Then a man sitting next to him asked, with great respect, "Jeshua, you use the words spirit and soul as if they are separate. Are they not one and the same?"

"No," Jeshua responded, "they are not. The spirit is eternal and immortal, for indeed it is part of God. But the soul, the soul is forever changing. It is the personality of the spirit, the intellect and the emotions of the spirit. It is forever changing with each new experience that you have. You are a manifestation of your soul that is constantly competing with the challenge of your mortal desires and wants, which may be in conflict with your soul."

Another then asked, "So, you are saying that the body is separate from the soul. But how can we separate the two, since are we not one and the same?" Jeshua answered, "You are not a mortal who by coincidence has a spirit and soul. You are a spirit with a soul that is having a mortal experience."

A great quiet came upon the group. Saul looked at his fellow listeners, who seemed to be acting so different from their usual behavior. There were not the usual interruptions, the cynical retorts and the confrontations taking place. Instead, everyone in the audience was listening with tremendous respect, trying to take possession of every word, as if they were treasures being handed to them.

Jeshua then broke the silence by announcing, "I must leave you now. I have other matters to attend to, but I am grateful for being able to visit with you." One of the men then asked, "Is it possible that you could come back tomorrow and visit with us again? We would greatly appreciate it if you could."

Jeshua looked at the man and smiled, "Yes, I will be back tomorrow. I will look forward to seeing you then." He then looked up at Peter and Andrew, who were seated behind Saul and the others, and beckoned them to come join him. Jeshua then smiled again at the group and raised his hand in farewell, as the two brothers nodded and the three of them turned and headed in the direction they had come from and turned the corner towards the gates. When they were out of hearing distance, Jamin said with great excitement, "Didn't I tell you, you would enjoy his words? Doesn't he have wonderful information that he can share with us?"

One of the other men responded, "There is something different about him. I can't describe it in words, but he is very unusual." Saul listened with great amusement as the group discussed the man from Capernaum. There was not one critical statement made, which Saul thought was extraordinary, considering the sarcasm and cynicism that was usually expressed among this group against others or themselves.

As Saul left the grounds of the Great Temple, and walked slowly through the market place and bazaar, he was deep in thought. Indeed, there was something extraordinary and unusual about this man Jeshua. Saul was certainly familiar with the expression love at first sight.

He was puzzled over his feelings towards this stranger, for he was indeed feeling love towards this individual, not the type of love that a man feels for a woman, but the type of love that a man feels towards a person who he holds in deep respect and who would be

very special to him.

Saul accepted that he was feeling a tremendous affection towards Jeshua, and that his presence as well as his words were having a tremendous impact on him. As he casually climbed the hillside back towards his home, he felt a wonderful excitement and anxiety within himself, as he anticipated meeting with his colleagues and Jeshua the next day.

Chapter 9
The Temple Gathering

The morning of the next day, Saul visited all three of the stalls that he had rented to his tenants in the marketplace. He intentionally was trying to occupy his mind in order to allow the time to go by as quickly as possible until he returned to the Great Temple to hear the words of Jeshua. He realized, as he visited with his renters, that he was just going through the motions of asking them questions, and sharing pleasantries.

This day was a cloudy day, and was cooler and more comfortable than most of the other days in mid-summer. The marketplace was crowded with thousands of people shopping, visiting with friends, seating at the outdoor restaurants, enjoying breakfast or just entertaining themselves. After his visits with his tenants, Saul then

walked to the well that was located in the central part of the marketplace and sat on the short round stone wall that surrounded the well, where he watched the activities with great amusement.

He could hear the epiphany of the many voices yelling out selling their wares, some with accents from other parts of the world. He saw women walking with baskets on their heads, and marveled at their ability to maintain its balance. He would occasionally see two or three Roman soldiers walking by, and people moving aside in different directions, leaving them a wider path then they did others. He recognized that most of the people that were visiting the bazaar were Judeans. He could also recognize by their faces and their clothing a sprinkling of others who were Syrians, Persians, Arabs, Phoenicians and Egyptians.

Saul eventually made his way over to the bazaar and chose a small table with a seat, where he ordered a light lunch consisting of white fish, boiled cabbage, dates, and some goat milk. Upon completing his meal, he began to make his way easterly in a direction of the Great Temple.

Upon his arrival at the portico at the north side of the temple, he noticed with interest that the usual number of people had increased from nine to over twenty.

Obviously, many of the individuals that had been there yesterday had invited friends to join them, which gave a different flavor to the group collectively. Friends were now talking amongst themselves, as opposed to people talking to the group collectively, as they were waiting for the arrival of the man from Galilee.

Saul seated himself on the sixth step, next to one of the regular participants of their daily discussions, and they began to chat informally. Not too much time had passed, when three men turned the corner of the temple, and were approaching the small crowd. There was Jeshua, dressed in the same attire as he had worn the day before, as well as the two brothers who were walking on his right.

Upon reaching the group, the two brothers continued walking up the stairs, seating themselves several steps behind the people that had already gathered. Jeshua stopped in front of the group, standing on the slab of marble below the first step. He looked at the group with a pleasant look on his face, his eyes making contact with almost each individual for a short time, before he smiled and said "How are you today my friends? I truly hope you are all well."

Different members of the group responded with their own greetings and salutations, which was a custom in this part of the world. A salutation such as how is your health, was not meant to be taken literally, but was a form of greeting that was customary. After the exchange of these pleasantries, one of the men in the group then asked

"Jeshua, may we hear your opinion to one of the questions that has challenged people throughout the ages? What is the purpose of life? I am the husband of a wonderful woman, the father of two children, and I am a tailor by profession. Is my purpose in life to be a devoted husband, or a loving parent, or to be an accomplished tailor? For I don't see myself becoming the governor of Judea, or a member of the Sanhedrin or an accomplished musician. So what am I supposed to accomplish during this lifetime before I die?" Another voice called out "Or is being born just an accident, and there is no

purpose to life?"

Jeshua listened to the question with great attentiveness. While the questions were being asked, although Jeshua was facing the person that was talking, his head was slightly bent and his eyes were fixed on the marble floor just in front of his feet. When the questions were finished, Jeshua continued for several seconds, appearing in deep thought. He then raised his head and first looked directly at the person who initiated the question, and then at the rest of the audience.

He answered "Every one of you are on a journey during your lifetime. The destination of the journey is to become at one with your father, who created you and who you are a part of, just as surely as the spirit of the Lord resides within you". He continued "Although your destination is the same, no two journeys are alike. It is you who decides how you wish to live your life while you are on this journey. Do you wish to be a tailor, or do you wish to be a musician? Do you wish to be married and have children, or remain unmarried? Do you wish to be a person who takes your journey with great seriousness, who is constantly looking for problems to solve and when solved, looks for new problems, or do you wish to be a person who lives life lighthearted without conflict? Do you prefer being a person who practices great generosity or a person who tries to accumulate wealth solely for your own benefit? You are the one who decides how you wish to live your journey".

"But Jeshua, what do we find at the end of our destination of this journey, and again, what is the purpose of this journey?" asked one of the listeners. Jeshua responded, "Your purpose and your destination are one and the same. It is to become at one with that part of God that resides within you, as I originally stated. You must envision within your own mind, that indeed, God does reside within you. Pretend that within each of you there is a temple, which has a thousand steps, and at the very top of the temple, God is waiting for you. As we go through our journey, our purpose is to continue to ascend the steps higher and higher, closer and closer to God, until indeed we reach the top step and become one with God.

"Just as no two people take the same journey, also no two people are on the same step. Some people unfortunately may be on a very low step or some may be in the middle, and there are others who are close to reaching the top. You know who those are, for you can tell by their behavior, their value systems and the level of compassion that they show their brothers and sisters, at what point of their journey that they are on."

A listener called out "Jeshua, how does one accomplish going higher and higher up the stairway? Are there specific things we must do, such as the amount of time that we spend in the Great Temple praying, or giving tithing's to the priests? What enables us to climb higher up the stairway to become one with God?"

Saul was enthralled with the answers that Jeshua was giving to these questions. He noticed the incredible respect that was being given to this man from Capernaum, and the effect that his words were having on the people that had gathered to listen to him speak. He also noted that a few other people had joined them that had been passing by the portico, and had also heard the words of Jeshua and decided that they too wanted to be the beneficiary of his wisdom.

After almost twenty seconds had gone by, Jeshua then looked up from the ground at his audience and answered "No, tithing will not earn you a position closer to God, for you cannot buy your way into his presence. Nor does it matter how many hours that you spend within the Great Temple praying, because your bodies are a living temple of God and you are able to pray at any time you choose, no matter if you are in a field, in your place of work, or in your home. It is through acts of love, acts of kindness and generosity that you find yourself becoming closer to that part inside of you that is God, that you are ascending the stairs.

"But by the same token, if you commit acts that are injurious to others, if you create fear in others, or hurt others by your words or deeds, then shall you find yourself descending the stairs, and become further removed from God." Another in the crowd then asked, "Is there one particular way that is better than another in order to try to become one with God as quickly as possible?"

Jeshua answered "No, there is not one particular way, but there are many roads that lead to the house of God. Nor is there one sect of the Judaic religion that is more favorable than another. It doesn't matter whether you are a Pharisee, or a Sadducee or an Essene, or even one who prays to a lemon tree, but it is your personal relationship with God that will enable you to enjoy life in great abundance, regardless of your wealth or lack of wealth, regardless of the road that you choose on this journey."

"Jeshua, what if you don't reach the top of the stairs in this lifetime? What then will be the outcome of not having reached your destination?" asked another. Jeshua responded "Life does not begin with your birth and end with your death. Your spirit is immortal and everlasting. Whatever level that you are on when your spirit leaves this present life that you are experiencing, will be that same level that you will continue on in your journey. But you, and only you can choose how quickly you reach your destination, and our father encourages you to help others in also having them reach their destination."

A voice from the crowd asked, "But Jeshua, what you are sharing with us is not consistent with what we are told by the priests. We are taught in the temples that we can't find God without the aid and help of the priests. Are you not refuting their teachings?"

"If one were to travel from here to Bethlehem, there are many different ways in order to make this journey. Some of you may choose to walk, others may choose to ride a donkey, others a camel and still others may decide to ride on a horse. The method you choose will certainly allow some to get from Jerusalem to Bethlehem faster, particularly if you ride on a horse as opposed to if you are walking. But is it not true, regardless of what method you use, that indeed you will eventually find yourself in Bethlehem?"

"And the same is true regarding those that you choose to be your spiritual guides. I do not discourage you from receiving the help of those who teach at the temples, but nor do I tell you that it is a requirement in order for you to be at one with God. But I will say to you with all the certainty in my heart, that God does not care about rituals, that God does not care about sacrifices of animals in his name, and in fact does not want you to kill innocent animals in his name. And God does not care about your tithing, because you cannot

purchase your way into the house that God lives in."

A murmur was heard through the small crowd. And then there was total silence for a considerable amount of time, as people were allowing their intellect and their hearts to absorb the words of the man from Galilee. Saul was totally enthralled with the information that Jeshua was sharing. It was so profound thought Saul, yet at the same time so simple. The priests and the Sanhedrin may not agree with the words that Jeshua had just spoken, but indeed it certainly made sense.

The Sanhedrin was a group of seventy men, some that were Pharisees and others that were Sadducees, even though the Pharisees were the majority. These men had been appointed as a council that controlled and managed the temples and decided which priests were to serve at which temples. The members of the Sanhedrin were men that had been appointed for life, and only upon their death, or if they resigned as a result of poor health, were they then replaced with another.

Not only was it the responsibility of the Sanhedrin to control the system of justice in Jerusalem, pertaining to minor crimes such as theft, the defaulting on the payment of debts, trespassing, and other violations of this nature, but the Sanhedrin also determined if a person who was accused of blasphemy, indeed was guilty of violating and defiling the name of God or committed an act in defiance of God.

If there was a matter of a capital crime, such as murder or treason, only the Romans were allowed to prosecute the person accused of that crime as well as to decide to execute the penalty that was imposed against those who were found guilty, whether it be death or imprisonment. In listening to Jeshua's words, Saul didn't feel that Jeshua was committing blasphemy, but his teachings would certainly not be well received by the Sanhedrin or their priests.

Following an unusually long silence, Jeshua apparently recognized that this was the appropriate time to end the discussion. He motioned for his two followers to come down from the stairs and join him on the marble slab at the base of the first step. The audience recognized that this was his way of letting people know that he was now prepared to depart. Saul immediately rose from his seat and hurriedly walked down the steps to catch up with Jeshua, who was now walking with his two followers towards Saul's left. Saul caught up with him just prior to them turning the corner.

"Jeshua, may I speak to you for a moment?" Saul asked. Jeshua stopped and turned to Saul with a loving smile on his face. He didn't say anything, but looked into Saul's eyes, and again Saul had the feeling as if be could see into his soul. "Is it possible that you will have any time that I may have a private conversation with you?" Saul asked.

"I will be leaving Jerusalem in two days, but if you wish, I could meet with you early tomorrow evening, and we could talk at that time. Is that convenient for you?" Jeshua responded.

"Yes. Tomorrow evening would be fine. Where shall we meet?" Saul asked. "At the outskirts of Jerusalem, just before you take the road that leads to Bethany, there is an inn on the right hand side of the road as you are facing the direction of Bethany. Why don't we meet outside of the inn at sundown?" Jeshua suggested.

Saul smiled and nodded his head in agreement. "I will be there Jeshua. I look forward to the time we'll spend together," Saul answered. Saul then looked at the two companions of Jeshua, who were both staring at him blankly. Their faces were without expression, but he could not see friendship in their eyes. They appeared to resent Saul's request to meet with Jeshua, as if it were an intrusion. But Saul didn't care. He could only feel excitement within him, in anticipation of being able to visit with Jeshua on such a personal basis.

Chapter 10
Gamaill

The following morning Saul awoke with Jeshua strongly in his thoughts. He continued to hear the words in his mind; over and over again that Jeshua had shared the previous afternoon at the temple. Where was this man getting his tremendous wisdom? How is it possible a person who had grown up along the Sea of Galilee, in Capernaum, would have this knowledge and understanding? These were just some of the thoughts, as he lay in bed, before starting his day.

After Saul got dressed and had a light breakfast, he decided to visit a mentor of his, a rabbi named Gamaill, who was considered one of the most educated and intelligent Pharisees in all of Jerusalem. Saul had developed a relationship with Gamaill since his

arrival in Jerusalem several years ago, and held him in tremendous respect.

Many times the two would sit for hours in Gamaill's house or along the table and benches in the shade of one of the trees in his yard and have in depth discussions regarding interpretations of the Torah, as well as other areas dealing with religion and spirituality, in addition to philosophy.

Gamaill was very fond of Saul, and was delighted whenever he visited with him. He recognized that Saul was not only well educated but also a person of very high moral values as well as exceptionally intelligent. He enjoyed asking Saul questions, for often times he would have an insight on a particular subject that Gamaill hadn't previously considered.

Saul arrived at Gamaill's house at mid morning, which was located approximately a ten-minute walk northwest of where the Great Temple was located. It was a neighborhood of older homes, that were not large or luxurious, but the houses as well as the properties were well maintained and were held in high regard. Many of the people in Gamaill's neighborhood were employees that worked at the Great Temple.

When Saul arrived he found Gamaill sitting outside, in his favorite spot underneath the shade of several large trees, drinking from a large goblet that was filled with warm milk. There was also a tray of honey cake and dates. As Saul walked through the gates of his front yard, and began to walk to his right up the slightly sloped front, he and Gamaill both broke into smiles. "Saul, my dear young man. It's so good to see you," shouted Gamaill with glee.

Saul didn't respond until he had seated himself on the bench across the table from Gamaill. He then said, "I hope that I'm not bothering you. I'd like to talk to you about some experiences that I've had in the last few days that are of great interest to me." Gamaill responded, "Certainly, certainly. I always have time for you Saul. It's always a pleasure to see you. What's on your mind?" Saul looked at Gamaill with great intensity before he began. He truly felt a great deal of respect and love for this elderly man, whom he knew was not in particularly good health.

Gamaill was very short and robust in build, with a bulging waistline that was visible even under his loose fitting robe. His face almost resembled that of an owl, with large brown eyes, a balding head and a close-cropped beard that was a combination of gray and reddish brown. His eyes revealed both wisdom and love, and Saul felt a great deal of affection towards him as he began to share his thoughts.

"A man had joined us at our daily talks at the temple, and his words have had a great impact on me. He is a Galilean, from Capernaum and he's giving us new information. He's visited with us twice in the last several days, and his words have had a profound effect on me," Saul began.

Over the next twenty minutes Saul described in detail the questions as well as the answers that Jeshua had provided to them. He intentionally avoided giving his own interpretations and impressions and tried to be as factual as possible. Gamaill listened with tremendous interest, without interrupting Saul even once.

When be was through, Gamaill spoke "Galilee is a very

interesting place, Saul. In many ways it is not too different than the province of Samaria, which does not practice Judaism the same as most of us do in Jerusalem. Over six hundred years ago when the northern kingdom of our country of Israel had experienced destruction, there were five Babylonian tribes that were transferred to that part of our land.

The people from those tribes eventually accepted Judaism, and intermarried with Jews, but obviously, they produced future generations of children that were not as orthodox as those of us in Jerusalem." Gamaill stopped for a while, giving Saul an opportunity to absorb what he was saying. He then continued to speak,

"But as you may know, in Galilee, along the western shore of the Sea of Galilee, there are many who are political activists, but it also has been a fertile breeding ground for holy men. And as you know Saul, it is not under the occupation of the Romans, but it's presently administered by Herodian, Tetrach and then they have the zealots, who we also know as the Galilean brigands, who come down to Jerusalem and try to incite the people to rise up against the Romans. Yes, Galilee is a very interesting area.

"But this man you speak of, Jeshua, I have not heard of him. But occasionally we know there are those individuals who travel throughout the three provinces of our country preaching or teaching that they have a special relationship with God, and have knowledge that no one else has." Saul then spoke, "But he didn't make any remarks of that nature. He spoke with great humility, and you could feel his respect and love for those he was talking to. It wasn't as if he was preaching to us, for his style was more that of a teacher. But there was something very special about him. But Gamaill, what of his words? What is your interpretation of his words that he shared with us, and also even though it's not as important, how did he know that my father's name was Zerah?"

Gamaill answered, "Saul, isn't it written in the great book that there are those who are prophets of God? God has given the gift of prophecy and understanding to very few individuals, but indeed they have existed throughout time. Apparently, Jeshua may be one of these prophets. But you ask me for my interpretation of his words. How can I find fault with one who speaks of compassion, love and kindness? If instead you told me was trying to motivate the people to pick up swords and fight the Romans, instead I would say, ah, another Galilean zealot."

Gamaill continued "As a Pharisee Saul, isn't it our responsibility to continually challenge the interpretations of other's words in order to have a greater understanding of the laws of Judaism? Almost thirteen hundred years ago, when Moses lead our forefathers out of slavery from Egypt, didn't we think of God at that time as being instrumental in helping the Jews fight the battles and to win their wars? In other words, our God at that time was a military leader, but then years later, when Moses brought the Ten Commandments to the people while they were in the desert, did we not interpret God as trying to instill goodness and morality into our people?"

"When your Jeshua speaks of the spirit of God being inside of us and climbing the steps of a temple, it reminds me of the teachings of my wonderful grandfather, Hillel the Great. He shared with me that too many people think of themselves as a vessel, wanting to be

beautiful on the outside so they might look visually good, but they forget it's more important that their real beauty be inside. There are too many people who try to give the appearance of observing the laws, but they do not have the true spirit in their heart."

Saul then asked, "But Gamaill, how do we respond to information which is in conflict to that which we have already been taught? Some of the things that Jeshua told to us are not consistent to what the priests have told us in the past." Gamaill looked directly into Saul's eyes and leaned his body and head over the table to be closer to Saul's face.

He then answered with great earnest "Should we believe everything that we are exposed to as truth? Should we believe the dogma and other information that has been given to us through the ages as automatically also being truth? No Saul, we shouldn't assume that because something has been told to us many times that it is truth, even if it is coming from those who claim to be the religious authorities. But it's only after we carefully consider and evaluate what is being told to us, and we determine if it is reasonable and logical, and that it is beneficial to us who are exposed to it, only then should we accept it and live by it."

Saul then asked "So you don't find fault in the words that Jeshua shared with us?" Gamaill responded, "Saul, there are many people who are absolutely committed to their own perspective of what is right and what is wrong. When they are exposed to conflicting views, they will choose the information which is consistent with their own belief system and will reject that which is not consistent with their own beliefs. So with your friend Jeshua, it may be very difficult in having others accept his perceptions, which have already been trained to reject information which is not consistent with their understanding of what is truth."

Saul listened carefully to the words of Gamaill. As always, this very respected and famous rabbi of Jerusalem was sharing profound wisdom with him. Saul would have liked to continue with the conversation, but he recognized that Gamaill was growing weak and he didn't want to be a physical burden on his elderly friend. Saul stood up from his seat on the bench and walked around the table to Gamaill. The elderly man stood up and the two of them embraced in an affectionate manner and then said their goodbyes.

As Saul started to walk down the gentle hill from the home of Gamaill, he felt that he still needed others to talk to, so he could try to reach down into his own soul to discover his own inner thoughts and his own heartfelt feelings over what he was experiencing. He couldn't quite place his finger on it, but he felt that only in conversation and in asking questions and perhaps answering some of his own, would he be able to release these unusual emotions that he was feeling inside which were unfamiliar to him and he couldn't quite identify. These were his thoughts as he continued his walk downhill towards the bazaar and marketplace, to join several friends for lunch.

Chapter 11
The conversation

Saul worked his way through the market place among the many stalls and the throngs of people doing their late morning shopping. The weather on this day was sultry, and Saul was dressed in a lightweight tunic. He wore a belt that was made of Egyptian rope that was loosely tied around his waist. The hem of his skirt ended just above his knees and he was wearing sandals with low cut straps that ended just above the ankle.

Saul approached the table where two of his friends were sitting, which included his very large friend Aaron, whom he had lunch with two days earlier. They had selected a table which was shaded with the same material which was used for making tents that was suspended over their heads by poles, providing shade to several

tables, one being where Aaron and Saul's other friend were already seated. Saul smiled at the two men, as he approached their table and sat down in the chair opposite Aaron. "Greetings to you Aaron, and to you also Shelah. I hope today finds you well" said Saul.

Shelah answered, "How could I not be well? Haven't you heard that I have found a container of gold in my backyard last night as I was digging a pit for my cistern?" Saul didn't respond and only laughed. Shelah was known for his humor and lighthearted manner in which he viewed life. Saul noted that Shelah was dressed in an odd looking outfit, in which it appeared he intentionally selected colors that didn't match, between his upper garment and his skirt. His tunic was of black and white stripes, running almost in a vertical direction, and his skirt was purple. On his head he wore a scarf that had been tied in back, which was multicolored. It occurred to Saul that his odd selection of clothes was intended to draw attention to himself, as was his harmless humor.

Aaron was wearing the same outfit that he had worn the last time they had visited and as always, had a large smile behind his unkept bushy beard. Saul realized that the friendship between Aaron and Shelah was mainly due to the light hearted manner of both of them, appearing to take life lightly on the surface, although Saul knew that below the smiling exterior of Aaron, was a person of high intelligence and a fine mind.

Saul noted there were four drinking vessels made of clay set on the table, and a large clay pitcher of spiced wine. "Is someone else joining us?" he asked. "Yes, yes" answered Shelah. "Your best friend Nadob will be joining us. As always, he will bring you great happiness with his sunny personality and wonderful disposition," laughed Shelah. Saul smiled in response to his remarks. Nadob was a person with a very cynical nature, who had a tendency to always look at the negative side of every issue. Saul did like him as well as his other two friends already seated, but Nadob was certainly not a person that you would want to find yourself alone with in a crisis, when you're looking for someone to inspire you to find a solution.

Then Aaron spoke up. "Let's not eat until he joins us. He should be here soon." The three men talked casually, while they were waiting for the arrival of Nadob. Aaron amused his two friends with stories of his two children and some of the clever sayings that surprisingly came out of the mouth of each child as they were learning their way through life.

Within a very short period of time, Nadob joined the three men at the table. He was wearing a very dark grey robe just several shades lighter than being black that fell halfway down his calves. On his head, he wore an embroidered skullcap, for he was very orthodox in his religious beliefs. Nadob was the only one of the four that was a Sadducee, where as Aaron and Saul practiced the Pharisee sect of Judaism. On the other hand, Shelah didn't profess to any religious belief. He was like a number of people that lived throughout Israel, that were Jews by their bloodline, descendants from one of the twelve tribes of Israel, but didn't observe the religion.

As Nadob sat down at the empty seat, he looked up at his three companions and said, "Well, I see the three of you are still alive. Apparently the Romans haven't yet discovered your plots to overthrow them. What poisoned food are we going to eat today?"

Shelah responded "Aaron, why don't you order for all four of us, and we'll share the food together. Who would be a better expert of food then our good friend Aaron as evidenced by his bountiful stomach?"

The three men chuckled as Aaron pushed himself away from the table and walked over to the food stalls. He visited two different places side by side and shortly afterwards several large plates of foods were delivered to their table which included spicy meat wrapped in grape leaves, pomegranates, green and black olives, aged goat cheese and a plate of various vegetables which included cabbage and artichokes. The four men began to serve themselves from these platters onto their individual plates as Saul began the discussion.

Saul proceeded very carefully to tell his companions of his experience in the last several days, trying to again share with them the facts without expressing his own impressions or judgments. When he was through, Nadob spoke up. "Just what the world needs, another zealot, to confuse the people and to give them false hope."

"No, I disagree with you," responded Aaron. "I believe this man Jeshua may have something very important to say. Isn't happiness the quest of all people? Aren't we trained to believe that happiness is directly related to the satisfaction of our material needs? Aren't people often judged by their peers, by the size and the cost of the homes that they live in, the clothes that they wear and the number of servants they have waiting on them?"

"Indeed, that is the case," answered Shelah. "And that's why Aaron, you will never be the envy of any of your peers," laughed Shelah. "But don't you see" responded Nadob the cynic. "This man says happiness has nothing to do with material things, but don't the poor have envy and hostility towards the wealthy? Isn't it a constant struggle for those who are poor to also want to live in the right neighborhood, to want to provide private education for their children even though they can't afford it? These are goals that can only be achieved through having the wealth to buy these things, and this man, Jeshua says it has nothing to do with happiness?"

Saul responded "Jeshua says happiness is the joy found in relationships that we have with others. He says that is the way we should live our lives, to be able to learn to enjoy life every day and let others enjoy life through us." "Well" said Shelah with a big smile, "as far as climbing the temple, Aaron you will never make it to the top. You will die from exhaustion before you get halfway up."

Saul continued pressing his three friends for their comments. The three personalities were so different, that he was able to get a totally different perspective, from Shelah who thought life was a series of laughter, Aaron, who appeared to be tremendously impressed by the information that Saul shared with them, and Nadob, who tried to find something negative in his responses to the comments of his colleagues.

The four men sat there for a long time, having finished their meal, and continued to order more spiced wine. It was now mid-afternoon and they began to say their farewell, in order to continue with their personal daily activities. "Saul," said Nadob, "don't place too much of your energy into this man. He sounds like he might be a troublemaker. Regardless of any anger that he may create with the priests, the last thing that the Romans want is to have a Jew from

along the Sea of Galilee to create confusion in Jerusalem."

Aaron responded "No, you are wrong Nadob. The Romans don't care what we do with our religion. They only care that they collect their taxes on time and in the amounts that they demand." Saul looked at Shelah to see his response, but he had none. He only smiled as he stood up and shrugged his shoulders. The three men concluded their farewells, discussing a schedule as to when they would meet again for lunch and continue in their conversations and then they all turned to leave.

Saul continued walking through the bazaar, so he could visit one of his stalls before returning home, and the others left in their own directions. Saul walked very slowly with his hands clasped together behind his back, as he worked his way through the crowd. He was truly oblivious to all the activity around him, for his mind was still totally engrossed in thoughts regarding Jeshua and the responses of not only his friends that he just shared the last several hours with, but also the profound remarks that Rabbi Gamaill spoke earlier in the day.

When Saul reached his house, he went directly to his personal chambers located on the east wing of the residence. He had no intent of eating dinner because of the large lunch he had just shared with his friends. Instead he spent most of the evening reading from several scrolls, and after the sun had set in the evening and the dark of the night had arrived, Saul went outside to the front yard and sat on the bench overlooking the city.

Saul thought again of the words that Jeshua had shared with them. If indeed, we are all on a journey to the same destination, and the quality of the journey will differ greatly with each individual, he asked God that his journey be filled with harmony as opposed to chaos or confusion. He thought to himself, that indeed the most important thing that he must embrace and totally accept in his own life is that we are all part of God. Isn't this what distinguishes us from any other living thing on earth, that within each of us, as Jeshua said, is the spirit of God which provides us with our immortality?

Saul continued to process his thoughts. Because a part of God is inside of us, it gives us tremendous power, but also gives us tremendous responsibilities that mankind is not always able to handle. Man gives life, Saul thought, but man also takes life. Man plants a tree and man cuts a tree down. Man breeds animals, and man kills animals. Unfortunately Saul thought, man is able to create, but man is also able to destroy. He concluded that if only man was able to understand and accept the responsibilities of being a part of God, surely we would live in a world that would indeed bring us greater happiness and joy.

Chapter 12
Bethany

Saul had a very light supper before he began his descent down the hill in a north-easterly direction. When he eventually reached the flat land, he continued walking north to where the road to Bethany began, which took him approximately thirty minutes from his house. The inn at the beginning of the road to Bethany was located on the eastern side of the road.

Saul arrived just before sundown, and waited across the road under a cluster of olive trees. He kneeled on his haunches and leaned back against a tree, watching people going by in both directions. The inn not only catered to those people that were traveling between Bethany and Jerusalem, but also a popular establishment where people visited for a quiet meal or for drinks and conversation as

opposed to traveling to the bazaar, where it was crowded and noisy.

Not too much time had passed when Saul saw Jeshua approaching with one of the brothers that had been introduced as Peter several days earlier at the temple. As they reached Saul, he stood up, walked several steps in their direction and greeted them. Jeshua returned the greeting with a smile, and turned to his companion and said, "Why don't you go ahead and I will meet you at Mary's. We'll be walking very slow, so don't concern yourself as to how long it will take me to join you. Just tell them that I am on my way."

Peter turned to Saul, casting an unfriendly look in his direction and without saying another word began to walk in an easterly direction, with his back to Jerusalem. Bethany was only a short distance, an approximate fifteen minute walk northeasterly from Jerusalem with Qumran and the Dead Sea, which at that time was known as the Salt Sea, approximately a half hour walk due west.

It was a clear day with just a few white billowy clouds scattered above. The weather was comfortable at this time of late afternoon, and Saul and Jeshua began to casually walk in the direction of Bethany. Jeshua asked, "Do you mind walking with me? I'm not going very far, just to the home of some dear friends that I had mentioned that live in Bethany, that were originally from Magdala."

Saul responded, "No, that's fine Jeshua. I have no plans for the rest of the day." Jeshua then turned to Saul, stopped and faced him, and again gave him that look that Saul felt went directly to his very soul. Jeshua said, "Saul, tell me about yourself. I can tell by your slight accent, that in addition to our native language in Israel, that your primary language is Greek. How is it that you are here in Jerusalem?"

Saul answered, "When I finished my education in Tarsus, I chose to come to the Holy Land to make my permanent home. I wanted to learn about our religion first hand, and wanted to live among fellow Jews, rather than continue in Tarsus. I feel that this is my home."

"What does your father do? I assume you came here with his blessings." As they continued slowly to walk towards Bethany, Saul responded, "He's a land owner who grows many products as well as the raising of animals to sell for food in the city. He inherited his wealth from his father, my grandfather whom I had never met, for I was born later in my parent's life. They migrated from northern Israel when my father was a young boy, and he did encourage and approve of me moving to Jerusalem. And you, Jeshua, what about your parents?"

Jeshua smiled, and hesitated for a few moments, he then said, "My parents? My father was a carpenter. He had a shop attached to the house where we lived and he repaired furniture that was broken. He would also buy used furniture, and refinish them to be resold, such as chairs or tables." Saul responded, "You say he was a carpenter. Has he passed on or has he retired from his work?"

"My father was considerably older than my mother when they married. She was sixteen and he was twenty years older. He passed on when I was a teenager, and my mother still lives in Capernaum in the same house I grew up in as a child," Jeshua answered.

Jeshua proceeded in explaining to Saul that he had traveled as a teenager away from home in order to pursue his own personal

studies, and that he had been gone at the time his father had become ill and had passed away. During this discussion of their personal lives, Saul also discovered that Jeshua was twenty-four years old, almost three years older than Saul.

As they continued their conversation, Saul noticed that the houses along the road to Bethany were quite far apart, sitting on very large properties which were farm land growing produce such as artichokes, cabbage, and many groves of olive and fig trees. They also came across houses that were obviously farms with different animals parading around, fenced in on the property. The topography was relatively flat, and certainly had a different atmosphere than the hubbub and exciting chaos of Jerusalem.

Saul then changed the topic of conversation. He stated to Jeshua, "I was tremendously impressed with what you shared with us the two times that you joined us at the temple. May I ask Jeshua, what are you trying to accomplish?" Again, Jeshua stopped walking and turned to Saul and answered, "I'm very concerned of what the religious leaders are teaching in the temples.

"In their effort to control people's lives, I feel they are pushing them further and further away from God. They appear to be more interested in rituals. I feel many times that the people can have a closer relationship and a greater understanding of their relationship with God, by their own efforts, as opposed to being pushed further away from God by what is happening in the temples."

"So Jeshua, do you see yourself as a spiritual guide for these people?" asked Saul. Jeshua responded, "If they choose to have me Saul, indeed I am willing to be their spiritual guide. But we all have spiritual guides that are with us throughout our lives. Even though people may not be aware of their presence, they are with you always.

"And you, Saul, I would encourage you also to communicate with your guides. If you don't communicate with them, this means that there's communication only one way, in that they are giving you information and you in turn are not responding or acknowledging them." They continued walking for a short while in silence, and then Jeshua said, "I don't suggest my friend, that you walk down the road talking to yourself. But I do suggest that you find quiet moments during the day when you are able to find peace at heart and peace of mind, and pray to them just as you pray to God. They are the messengers of God, and in being so, it's not in conflict with God for you to pray to your spiritual guides. They are your guardians and they have been assigned to you by God."

Saul was trying to absorb Jeshua's words, and at the same was deep in thought. He then asked, "So if I don't call upon them, they won't be with me? Is that my understanding of what you're sharing with me?" Jeshua answered, "Your guardians are with you always. They don't judge you and you don't have to be embarrassed for your mortal acts, and think they are inappropriate and would be looked down upon by your guardians.

"On earth our needs are substantially different than they are in the spiritual world, just as in the spiritual world, you do not have earthly needs. Unlike the spiritual world, when you feel hunger, thus you find the need to eat; when you feel thirst, then you have the need to drink. That is the law of nature and so being; you must never be embarrassed towards your guardians, the messengers of God, as you

satisfy your earthly needs. On the other hand, if you are performing acts which you would be embarrassed of other people knowing, that is another matter."

"But Jeshua," Saul responded, "you spoke to us at the temple that the spirit of God resides within us. What of that relationship? Should we listen to our spiritual mind as well as our guardians?" The two men continued walking slowly on the road to Bethany. Jeshua responded, "You should make a conscious effort to ask your spiritual mind as well as your guardians to bring you harmony, peace and love. Your spiritual mind and your spiritual guardians will provide you help and guidance for what you ask, although the final results are really up to you."

Jeshua continued, "Some of the time you may wish to communicate with your thoughts, speaking in silence to your eternal partners. Other times in the privacy of your own home, or as you walk on the road or in the temple, you may wish to communicate with your spiritual mind and your guardians verbally. They will respond, as any good partner, to that which you ask. You must never use them for negative or selfish purposes, for your spiritual mind and your spiritual guardians will not respond to that which is harmful or self serving. But they will respond to that which you are entitled to, a life filled with love, harmony and happiness."

Saul responded, "Jeshua, I don't recall the priests in the temple telling us to pray to anything other than to God. Are they wrong, for you're saying that it is appropriate for us to also pray to our spiritual guides, and to our own spiritual being? Is that not in conflict with God?"

Jeshua smiled, and then waited a few seconds before he answered, "But Saul, they are all part of God. They are a part of God's family, and are a part of God. If you were to eat an olive from a tree, is it not part of the tree? If you were to drink from a goblet that has drawn water from a lake, is not the water you drink part of the lake? You cannot separate God's messengers from God, just as you cannot separate the children of God from God. We are all part of that same Oneness."

Saul had lost all recognition of how much time had gone by. He now realized that he and Jeshua had reached the house of Jeshua's friends. They were now standing on the road looking at a house that was sitting back from the road approximately forty yards with a makeshift fence going in either direction of the open gate onto the property. To their left and slightly in front of the house was a large outdoor table, with benches on either side. Saul could see that behind the house there were animals wandering around consisting of goats as well as hens. Seated on one side of the table were Jeshua's companion Peter and another man, and across from them was a woman dressed in a gray robe.

Jeshua turned to Saul and said, "Join me for awhile Saul, and let me introduce you to my friends," and without saying another word he opened the gate and walked onto the property towards the three seated people. Saul hesitated for a moment and then followed behind Jeshua.

The man seated next to Peter stood up, and then took several steps toward Jeshua with a big smile on his face and with his arms extended open in greeting.

He was a very tall thin man, with a narrow but long beard that came to a point. The hair on his head as well as his beard was peppered, in that it was a combination of dark gray and white, and on his head he wore a turban. The tall man stated "Jeshua, you have finally arrived. We were ready to go looking for you thinking that perhaps you had gotten lost," he said jokingly.

Jeshua smiled as he approached the man, and the two of them embraced. "Lazarus, I want to introduce you to my new friend, Saul of Tarsus." Jeshua then turned sideways to Saul, and said, "Saul, this is my dear friend whose family I have known for years. Lazarus, who is Magdalene, and that beautiful lady sitting there", as Jeshua gestured towards her, "is his sister Martha who is the greatest cook in Judea."

As Jeshua was speaking, a young woman came out of the house and approached them. Saul noted that she was extraordinarily striking in appearance, having long black raven hair, very large brown soulful eyes whose pupils almost appeared to be liquid, with dimples on both cheeks and a beautiful smile. Without saying a word, Jeshua turned towards her and the two of them came into each other's arms and gave one another a very affectionate and long embrace.

Jeshua then separated himself from the woman, holding his hands on both of her upper arms and said something to her that Saul couldn't hear. Jeshua's back was turned to Saul, but throughout this entire greeting, the woman had a beautiful loving smile on her face. Finally Jeshua looked over his right shoulder and said to Saul "Saul, here's my dear friend Mary, who is a sister of Martha and Lazarus."

During this entire introduction, Saul hadn't said a word. He now nodded acknowledging his introduction to Lazarus as well as to Martha. But he had difficulty taking his eyes off of Jeshua and Mary. He couldn't help but notice the affection that they appeared to have for one another.

Saul then said, "I must go now. Jeshua, may I talk to you for a moment?" The two men walked back towards the gate, side by side, and Saul then asked, "When will you be coming back to Jerusalem?"

"I'm not sure Saul. Perhaps in two months, possibly longer. But I'll leave a message for you at the stall that you described to me that you own, so that your renter will be able to tell you that indeed, I have returned. I'll also give them instructions as to where we can meet. I look forward to being with you and seeing you again when I return. Until then, may you walk in God's light."

This time the two men engaged in a farewell embrace, for Saul was now comfortable in feeling that they were no longer strangers. As Saul walked through the early evening back to Jerusalem and across the hill to his rented house, many thoughts went through his mind. He no longer had that strange feeling inside of the lower part of his stomach, which he had not been able to identify with prior to this evening, but instead felt a great deal of calm and harmony within his heart. He would truly look forward and count the days when he could spend time with Jeshua again, to learn more of the teachings of this man from Galilee.

Chapter 13
Reflections

Months would pass since Saul had last seen Jeshua. Saul would spend many hours in deep thought over the words that Jeshua had shared with him, both in person, as well as in his teachings at the Great Temple. He was trying to comprehend the impact that the man from Galilee had made on his life.

Saul understood how a person's life could be influenced by the teachings of another. Had he himself not had the benefit of some of the most intellectual and caring tutors during his youth in Tarsus? And certainly, had not Rabbi Gamaill made a profound impact on his life in providing greater understanding of Judaism and of the meaning of being a Pharisee? But Jeshua's words had penetrated beyond his mind, to the very core of his essence.

It had given him a totally different perception of his relationship

with God, as well as how he looked upon other people. No longer did he find himself judging people based on their standing in life, their wealth or their position. But instead, he found himself feeling a sense of love and affection towards all people and refraining from being judgmental.

Saul thought to himself "I shall love all people as my brothers and sisters until they give me a reason not to. And I shall have as much respect for the servant and the poor beggar, as I would for a person of authority or great wealth." These were his new thoughts and the new value system that had now become a part of Saul, as a result of the impact that Jeshua had on him.

Saul was not adverse to wealth, and certainly recognized the benefits, but neither was it an obsession with him. As a result of his training, his intellect and the financial base that had been given to him by his father, Saul knew that accumulated wealth would come easily to him. But outside of his interest in wearing clothing of high quality and being able to dine in the more expensive establishments, he had no other goals for his accumulation of wealth.

He had no ambitions to owning a luxurious villa or having servants, and neither did he have the same family interest as most men he knew his age that had been married by now, and were also involved in some form of manual labor hobby, in addition to their chosen profession.

Within the Judaic religion, particularly in Israel, manual labor was not considered a lowly position, but instead part of their way of life. It was very common for people of high intellect, such as teachers or rabbis, to also have another part time occupation such as a tailor, baker, or carpenter or to grow products on a small portion of land, not primarily to be a major source of income, but rather to express their humility and humbleness before God and their fellow men. But Saul, having grown up in Tarsus where he was more influenced by the Hellenistic Greek culture, didn't feel that need.

Saul would often give thought of trying to discover what were his goals and ambitions in life as opposed to the responsibility of providing for a wife and children. Not only did Saul not feel that need, but he also actually felt negative feelings in that regard, having grown up in a dysfunctional family, without loving and tender relationships between himself and his parents, as well as having witnessed the lack of affection in the relationship between his own father and mother.

As for his ability to accumulate wealth, he recognized that was more or less a fact of life, rather than a motivation or ambition, since he had no requirements to display the fruits of success as a badge of pride. So what then was to be his purpose?

He enjoyed his life, and certainly could continue on a daily basis indefinitely, participating in an active social life, increasing his business enterprises, engrossed in the time that he spent studying and reading interesting manuscripts, experiencing and reminiscing the passion that he shared with Leah and if necessary, other women. But still he recognized there had to be more important things in life that awaited him. Surely someday he would discover what they were.

It was on a quiet beautiful Sunday, approximately three months since the last time he saw Jeshua that he and Leah would meet Aaron and his wife Zelda for supper at a popular dining establishment a

short distance from the marketplace in Jerusalem.

When Leah and Saul arrived in the early evening, they found Aaron and Zelda already seated. Zelda, like Aaron, was a large person, with a round face and small mouth and pouting lips that always seemed to have a big smile that matched her round brown eyes. Saul reflected that they looked as if they were twins, in spite of their different genders.

Both Aaron and Zelda stood up as Saul and Leah approached the table and hugs were exchanged between the four of them, "Ah, what a perfect night to dine outside and to enjoy food, wine and conversation with dear friends," Aaron shouted. This evening was Saturday and the sun now having set, which ended the Sabbath; it was not uncommon in Jerusalem for friends to get together.

Then Zelda chimed in, "What's new? Do you have any exciting gossip or news to share with us?" Saul responded, "I hope that you have had a large lunch. I am sure that Aaron told you that last week we went to the races, and I had bet against Aaron, that his favorite runner wouldn't win. Unfortunately I lost, and I'll be paying for supper tonight. So please don't order very much food," he chuckled as he spoke. And indeed the previous Sunday Saul and Aaron had gone to watch the contests that were held between different runners, on the western side of the city near the large gymnasium. Both Aaron and Saul enjoyed sports and often would attend the wrestling matches and other sporting events together and Aaron had become quite proficient in selecting the winners.

"Quite contrary," responded Aaron. "We have fasted for two days and now are prepared to enjoy our winnings. Let us begin with the finest wine ever made in Damascus. Then we shall order our meal after we have tilted our cups a few times." Zelda chimed in "I will drink to that," and they all laughed together.

The evening continued with discussions of local gossip, each of the four taking turns sharing little tidbits of information as well as responding to each other's remarks. Towards the end of the evening when they had finished their meals and were enjoying a pleasant desert wine, Leah began to tell them of the daughter of her sister, her niece, and some of the cute remarks that she had said during a recent visit between the aunt and niece. When she had concluded Zelda said, "Leah, you're so beautiful, Saul just look at that face. What a beautiful wife and mother you'll make someday. Saul when are you going to make her an honest woman?"

Her question was answered in silence. A mask of sadness immediately appeared on Leah's face, as she cast her eyes downward. Saul just looked straight ahead, his face expressionless. Neither of them responded. After a period of awkwardness, Aaron broke the silence by saying that it was now time for them to say goodnight, and all four of them arose from the table and in the familiar style of expressing farewell, embraced and wished each other well.

Saul and Leah, without speaking, then walked over to three large men that were standing across the road, at the corner of two streets. They stood underneath a burning torch that had been dipped in oil and was held in place against the building through a bracket that had been driven in position by small iron spikes. This was the method of providing light at street corners, torches attached to buildings in the

evening in the heart of Jerusalem.

Saul hired one of the three that he had used previously, to act as a security guard for them. He would accompany them as they would walk up the hillside, the approximate twenty minutes to Leah's home. It was customary at that time, for people who could afford it, to hire a man to safeguard them as they walked through the streets in the evening in Jerusalem, to protect them from being accosted or robbed.

The security guards were not allowed to carry swords or knives, which would have been in violation of Roman law, but they indeed did carry a club that they either swung along side of them as they walked, or carried on their shoulder. They kept about four paces behind the person that had hired them, so they were outside of hearing distance so they didn't interrupt the privacy of their employer's conversation, but at the same time would be recognized as protectors if their employers were to be bothered.

Saul and Leah were almost totally silent as they walked up the hills towards the home of Leah, both of them still having been traumatized by the remarks of Zelda. When they reached the house, Saul paid the security guard. He then took Leah by the hand and they walked back towards the rear right hand side of her house, until they came to a grouping of trees.

Leah turned her back to one of the trees, and rested her shoulders against it, and the two of them were now facing each other. Rather than the normal intimate embracing and kissing that they had experienced in the past, Leah looked into Saul's eyes and said "Saul, what are we going to do? I am twenty years old, and most women my age are married by now, unless they are never to be married. I love you so much; I just don't know what to do. Why can't we live a life like others?"

Saul felt a tremendous pain within his heart. His love for her was not a question, but he knew that her maintaining her love for him was doing her a great injustice. If his love was selfish, he could continue with the relationship the way it was until one of them were to pass on in old age, but he knew that this was not right. He felt as if his very heart was being torn to asunder, as he looked into her beautiful eyes.

"I must release you Leah. It is unfair to you. I must help you go on. Please forgive, me," Saul whispered. Leah stood slightly on her tiptoes and placed her face along side of Saul's. Saul could feel the tears wetting both of their cheeks, but she didn't respond. Saul continued "Leah, you must find other men in your life. You must have other relationships, for you deserve to be the wife of somebody who can be the husband that you deserve, and to have the beautiful children that are waiting for you. Please forgive me, that I cannot be that person."

Saul removed his face several inches from Leah's so she would not feel the tears that were now running down his cheeks, the pain of knowing in his heart, within his soul, that he was losing that which he loved most in life, the only woman he had ever loved, for reasons he himself didn't comprehend, but knew it must be so. These were the last words they spoke to one another that evening; on the night that Saul had made a final decision that would affect him the rest of his life.

In the weeks, the months and the years to come, Saul would have many opportunities to be with other women. But whenever Saul did have an intimate relationship with a woman, there was an ache he felt inside the lower part of his stomach, that he experienced every time. He didn't understand the pain, which was almost like a hollow feeling, like a feeling of hunger, but it was always there during those intimate moments. Saul assumed that it was a feeling of guilt, something within himself that was acknowledging that he had hurt as well as denied himself the only woman that he had ever loved.

Later in life, as years went by, Saul would actually write letters to others, describing the anguish and heartache within him. Future letters he wrote to the people of Corinth as well as to the Romans would refer to the thorn in his side, the weakness of his flesh, and the constant fight within him between his sexuality and his spirit. But because he was a private person, although he referenced these painful experiences, he never explained why they existed or what caused them. *letting go of Leah whom he loved,*

Hundreds of years later, and yes, even two thousand years later, historians would still misinterpret his words of anguish. Some would assume that he had some malady, such as being crippled, or an abnormality in his looks, or some type of impairment. Even to his deathbed, Saul had never succeeded in winning over the conflict between his spirit and his flesh.

Chapter 14
Questions and Answers

More weeks would pass, with Saul continuing to feel the longing to spend time with Jeshua again. He had heard rumors that the Galilean had been in the Judea area since the last time they saw each other, but he couldn't confirm them. Saul continued his visits to the Great Temple, but never on the day of Sabbath or the day following the Sabbath.

Some of the other regulars would also ask if anyone had heard if Jeshua had returned to Jerusalem, and again, all they could talk of was rumors. None could actually confirm that indeed he had visited their city. Following his visits with them, they were now only meeting at most three times a week. They felt their meetings were not as relevant without Jeshua being there, for they didn't have the same depth.

Saul would also inquire at the temple he attended where he conducted his regular prayers on the Sabbath day. Although he occasionally visited the inside of the Great Temple, he was not comfortable in conducting his personal prayers in that magnificent setting, which he found very ostentatious and awe inspiring more then feeling his being in a religious sanctuary. Saul found the size of the temple and the temple grounds intimidating in some ways, although he occasionally watched activities of the priests around the Alter for Burned Sacrifices as well as the grandeur of the Holy Place, where the sacred scriptures of the Torah were kept.

Instead, Saul enjoyed praying at one of the many small temples scattered throughout Jerusalem, which catered to people of similar interests. The temple that Saul enjoyed visiting the most was located in the southwestern portion of the lower city, not far from the Pool of Siloam. It was one of a number of temples that had been started by people of the Jewish faith who had not been born in Jerusalem, but had migrated from other parts of the world.

There were a number of people that attended services at this temple that Saul attended that originally had been born in the Tarsus area, as had Saul, although he hadn't known them previously. Saul felt more comfortable attending services on a regular basis with others who had a similar Judaic background as Saul had received as a child growing up, in the Tarsus area. But at the same time almost without exception, he was more knowledgeable of the Judaic religion then his fellow worshipers, because of the special training he had the first three years he had been in Jerusalem, under the guidance of Rabbi Gamaill.

On this particular morning, we find Saul walking through the marketplace, having just visited two of the stalls that he owned. As he continued on his stroll, he noticed two women in front of him and to his right, that were studying some objects that were carved figurines that were being offered for sale at one of the stalls. As he approached them closer he realized that these were the same two women that he had met in Bethany, that were the sisters of Lazarus, that Jeshua had introduced to him the last time that they were together.

Saul approached the two ladies, whose backs were towards him, and hadn't yet seen him. When he got within several steps of them, he said, "Martha, Mary, do you remember me? It's so good to see you." The two ladies turned, and both immediately recognized him, and smiled. Martha spoke first saying "Of course. It has been quite awhile. We hope you are well." Mary added, "Saul, Jeshua spoke so highly of you after you left. It's so nice seeing you. Are you doing some shopping today?"

Saul responded, "No, I'm just visiting some stalls in which I have a business interest. Do you have time to relax with me and have a glass of spiced wine? I know of a nice place that we can sit and visit and chat. There are some questions that I would like to ask you." The two women looked at each other and both nodded their heads in the affirmative. Mary then said, "We would love to join you Saul. We're not in a rush. Let's sit and relax together and share a beverage."

Saul then lead them back in the direction that he had come, to an area which contained many restaurants and outdoor eating sections.

He observed as they were walking and engaging in small talk, that Martha was several inches shorter than Mary, and slightly robust. Although they didn't look like sisters, they had a similar smile, portraying their family resemblance. Mary was not only taller than Martha but much more graceful. She was slender and her hair was a black raven color, where Martha's was slightly lighter. She also had dimples on her cheeks, which Martha did not. But there was something about both of them that made Saul feel immediately at ease, as if they were old acquaintances.

When they had arrived at the outside eating area that Saul had lead them to, he then invited them to sit down. He then went to one of the stalls and ordered a pitcher of scented wine and some savory pastries. He returned to the table holding three goblets, with a young boy following him, carrying the pitcher of wine and the pastries on a platter, which he sat in front of them. Saul sat down and joined Martha and Mary. "I haven't seen Jeshua since that evening that I had met you. Has he returned to Jerusalem since then, or have you heard from him?"

Martha looked at Mary as if acknowledging that she would be the one that would answer. "Yes, Jeshua has been here twice since then. Once he did spend several days in Judea, in which he actually stayed at our home in Bethany, as our guest while he was here. Another time, he spent his entire visit in Judea, but mostly stayed in Bethabara where he was visiting a man that he's very close to whom preaches along the Jordan River."

Saul then blurted out; almost surprising himself by his own candid words "I feel a great deal of love for Jeshua. I really would like to know more about him if you're willing to share that with me." Saul looked a little embarrassed, feeling maybe his request was inappropriate. Martha responded "We would be glad to share information with you about Jeshua and please don't be embarrassed over the love you feel for him."

Mary added, "We also love Jeshua. I am sure that you realize that he's a very special person, very special." Saul responded, "Then let me start by asking you, did you know him when you lived in Galilee?" Martha answered "I'm sure you know that Jeshua and his family are from Capernaum, even though his mother and father were originally from Nazareth and they lived in Nazareth when Jeshua was born although he was not born in Nazareth. Jeshua spent his childhood as well as his early years of manhood in Capernaum, other than when he had gone away several years for his teachings."

Mary then continued "And our family is from Magdala, which is a short distance south of Capernaum. Saul, have you ever been in that part of Israel?" Saul responded, "No I haven't. I hope to someday, but I've never been there." Martha continued "There are a number of towns and small villages along the western shore of the Sea of Galilee, which the Romans call Lake Tiberius, after the Emperor Tiberius. But we Israelites still prefer to call the lake, the Sea of Galilee. It's not unusual for families to know each other that live along the Sea of Galilee, for it's not that large."

Saul asked, "How large actually is the Sea of Galilee?" Martha answered, "Well, Saul, as I said, it is actually a lake. It's about thirteen miles long and six miles wide, at its widest part. In fact, its widest part is between the western shore where we lived in Magdala

and on the shore of the town of Gergesa, which is of course on the eastern shore and is not in Israel, so we never go there. And most of the water that flows in the Jordan River actually comes from the Sea of Galilee." Saul then asked "So you knew Jeshua and his family when you lived in Magdala?"

Martha continued, "Yes, we did, but we were still young girls when we left Magdala, and moved to Bethany. Our brother Lazarus is quite a bit older than we are, and he certainly was a much closer friend to their family then we were, because of our ages. But yes, we did know Jeshua then, as well as his family, even though he himself was a boy when we lived in Magdala. And we said, he spent several years away for his schooling."

Saul asked, "What do you mean his schooling? He didn't attend classes while he lived in Capernaum?" Martha answered, "He spent several years in special training in the Essene colony in Samaria at Mt. Carmel. There was a special school there in the foothills of the southern portion of the mountain, not too far from the Great Sea. His mother Mary had also spent time there, when she was younger."

There was silence for a short while, while all three of them took several bites of the pastries in front of them, as well as took several sips of the scented wine. Then Martha continued "But they were not really Essenes. In fact, I'm not sure how you would describe Jeshua's belief system. Although we are all Jews, Jeshua is not an Essene, a Pharisee or a Sadducee. He really has his own belief system, which is very different from the traditional teachings of the different sects of our religion."

Saul nodded his head in affirmation, with a facial expression of deep thought and answered, "Yes, I know what you mean. Jeshua has spoken before me and others at the Great Temple, and also in my private conversations with him, and I agree, his belief systems are quite unique." Having heard those words, both Martha and Mary started laughing wholeheartedly. Martha added "Well that is one way of saying it, yes indeed. They are quite unique. There's no question, that he has a special relationship with God."

And, Mary added, "We would also like to have that same relationship, for that is his commitment in life, to help others to understand their special relationship with God, as opposed to the more conventional teachings of our religion, as taught by our religious leaders." Saul then stated, "I feel badly that I didn't get to see Jeshua when he was here last. I'd hoped that I would be able to spend some time with him, for there are so many things that I want to ask him about."

Martha responded, "Don't feel bad Saul. Jeshua is constantly going from one town to another town, one village to another village, back and forth between Jerusalem, down to Bethlehem, then up to Jericho, and then from Pharim, and all through the province to Samaria, as well as Galilee. I am sure that you will have an opportunity to see him many times in the future."

Mary then added, "Let me tell you of an incident that happened when he was here last, even though we didn't see it. Jeshua was walking with several of his followers, in the western portion of the old city, not too far from the Essene Gate, and came to a crowd of people shouting and waving their fists at somebody. When he approached them there was a woman who had her back up against

the wall, and these men had formed a half circle around her. They had rocks in their hands, and as it turned out, they were screaming at her that she was a harlot and were taunting and yelling ugly remarks at her."

Martha added "The woman had her face in her hands, and she was crying. Apparently she had either been caught or was being accused of having committed an act with a married man, and some wives were standing behind the crowd of men, yelling at the men to throw rocks at her as punishment." Martha's sister then said, "Like me, it turned out that this woman's name was also Mary. "

I was told by one of the men that was there that Jeshua pushed through the crowd and stepped in front of the woman, protecting her. He then stared at the men silently for a long, long time, and then said, "Which of you here have never committed a sin? I will say to each and every one of you, the one of you who has never committed sin, you be the one who throws the first stone."

Mary continued, "The men were stunned. They didn't know what to do. They just stood there as he stared into each one of their eyes. One by one, the men dropped the stones that were in their hands, turned and walked away, until Jeshua was alone with this woman. He then took her into his arms, and she sobbed on his shoulder, as he told her that she was forgiven, and that she should not sin any further."

All three of them now had tears in their eyes from the wonderful and touching story that had just been shared with Saul. After a few moments Saul then said, "I would have liked to have witnessed that. It must have been an incredible experience. I'm sorry that I couldn't have seen it." The three of them got their bearings together, and continued to enjoy their pastries and wine and Saul then said "Tell me about the two men that travel with Jeshua. What's their relationship, and who are they?"

Martha responded, "I am not sure which two men you mean. He has several men that follow him, who also are men who live in some of the towns and villages along the Sea of Galilee. There are two different sets of brothers, one that is called Peter and Andrew, who are from Bethsaida, which is almost at the very northern tip of the Sea of Galilee. Peter, who Jeshua sometimes calls Cephas, is a big, husky fellow with a bushy beard, who scowls a lot. His younger Brother is Andrew, who's a thinner, shorter man, almost beardless. He's gentler than Peter, and doesn't have as strong a personality as his older brother."

Mary then added "The other set of brothers are John and James, who are also fishermen, who are from Tiberius, which is just below Magdala, where we grew up. They work for their father who owns a number of fishing boats, who actually has a very large home also here in Jerusalem. I'm speaking of their father Zebedee that has the home." Martha then added "And there are several other men who also travel with him occasionally who are also from Galilee, along the western shores of the lake. They are all fishermen and they help Jeshua in a number of ways."

"What do you mean they help? What are their duties and responsibilities?" Saul asked.

"Well, they are his disciples. You know, his pupils," Martha answered. "They're not educated men and they don't have Jeshua's

wisdom, his knowledge, or his understanding. They are simple men, and they are learning from him."

Mary added, "Like you Saul, they love Jeshua and know he is a very special person. When Jeshua is traveling, they provide him companionship and safety. You know, it is not entirely safe for a person to travel by himself all the way from Galilee, through the province of Samaria to Judea. Usually, one or two will go ahead of the rest, and will find families that Jeshua and they can stay with when they arrive at the next town, with people who are willing to provide them with food and shelter during their stay."

Martha then added "In other words, they're committed to helping Jeshua and his mission, while at the same time they're trying to understand his teachings." Saul then asked, "You mentioned that there is somebody he visits along the Jordan River. Can you share with me information about those visits, or who he's visiting?"

Martha responded "First tell us about yourself Saul. It doesn't surprise me that you have all these questions about Jeshua, but tell us about you. Where are you from originally? I can tell from your mannerisms and your speech that you aren't originally from Jerusalem. We'd like to hear about you."

Saul then spent the next ten to fifteen minutes telling the two sisters about himself, about his childhood in Tarsus and the reasons why he left the region of Cilisia in order to come to the Holy Land. They also had many questions for Saul, which he listened to and carefully articulated each answer, so that they would realize he himself was willing to be as open with them, as they had been with him.

After they felt satisfied in knowing enough about Saul as they wished, and he had answered all their questions, Mary then said "Regarding Jeshua's visits to the Jordan River, his mother's sister, a woman by the name of Elizabeth, had a son who is about two years older than Jeshua. His name is John. He's strange in many ways. Although he and Jeshua are not tremendously close, there is still love between them.

John The Baptist

Mary continued, "John travels mostly along the Jordan River all the way south from the Salt Sea, north through Judea, into Samaria and preaches almost like a zealot to people he finds along the shores of the river." Martha then added, "Jeshua will visit with him from time to time, and will stay with John in the wilderness, where they will spend time together. As my sister said, John is very unusual, and doesn't like to live in the city, but prefers a very different style of living. But he is a preacher, and quite different than Jeshua, even though they are very bonded.

Perhaps sometime when you and Jeshua visit together here in Jerusalem, Jeshua will take you with him to the Jordan River, for it's not that far from here that John generally does his preaching, along the western shores of the river, near Bethabara." Martha now pushed away from the table and stood up, and said, "Now Saul, you know all you must know for now. If you have more questions, you can ask Jeshua. It's time for Mary and me to go about our business."

She said this with a loving smile on her face, and as Saul stood up, she walked over to him and gave him a hug. Mary also stood up and with that beautiful smile on her face and she also approached Saul and embraced him. "One last question please. You said that his

mother and father come from Nazareth. Is that where he was born?"

Mary answered, "He was actually born in Bethlehem. His mother and father had traveled down to Bethlehem, because of the required registration for taxes, and they arrived just prior to his birth. His mother Mary, another Mary," she laughed, "gave birth to him while they were there, which of course meant they had to remain another twenty-nine days by Judaic custom after his birth, before they could leave Bethlehem."

Martha added, "So, his parents were from Nazareth and that's why he is referred to as a Nazarene. But he was born in Bethlehem and was raised in Capernaum. It is interesting how life unfolds sometimes," she finished with a smile. Again, all three of them ended with the greetings consistent with their custom, then Martha and Mary turned back to the direction they had originally come from, towards the marketplace, and Saul began walking away from the lower city, up the hillside towards the upper city.

The two sisters had promised Saul that the next time Jeshua would visit Jerusalem that one of them would leave a message in the stall of one of Saul's renters that he had described in detail to them, as to where he could meet with Jeshua, so he wouldn't miss him again. As Saul slowly walked up the hill towards his home, he replayed in his mind the questions and answers he had shared with them during his visit with Martha and Mary.

He also replayed a scene in his mind of Jeshua having saved the woman Mary from being stoned by the angry crowd and tried to envision it as if he indeed had been there and saw the whole thing. "What an extraordinary man. I can't wait until I can again spend time with him," Saul thought as he walked the hills of the upper city.

Chapter 15
Jeshua Returns

Approximately two weeks after Saul's having unexpectedly met Martha and Mary at the marketplace, one very early morning he found a message waiting for him during one of his visits to the stalls. It was given to the tenant with whom he'd asked Mary to leave a message for him. His tenant told him that Mary and Martha had come by the previous afternoon and said that Jeshua had arrived in Judea yesterday morning and was staying with them. She had also said that Jeshua was looking forward to seeing him.

Saul felt a tremendous amount of excitement. He immediately walked to the small building in the northern portion of the marketplace in the lower city where you could hire boys who would deliver a message for you. He gave them directions to the home of

Lazarus and his two sisters, and he wrote a message on papyrus. He asked Jeshua if he could meet with them at their usual time that afternoon at the Great Temple.

Saul could hardly contain his joy as he saw the young boy place the papyrus in a cloth pouch, and jog his way through the marketplace in the direction of Bethany to deliver his message. Saul spent the rest of the morning trying to locate as many of people as he knew he could find that generally gathered at the Great Temple for their weekly discussions. He wanted them to know there was a possibility that Jeshua would be joining them that afternoon and they should invite other people who may have now heard of Jeshua who might also want to attend.

About three hours passed since Saul had sent his message to Jeshua, and he now made his way towards the Great Temple and felt a tremendous stir of excitement within himself. He hoped that Jeshua not only got the message, but would also be able to join them at the temple. In his excitement, he got to the temple earlier than he had anticipated. Rather than entering through the eastern gate to go to Solomon's Portico where they would be meeting, he decided to walk along the opposite side of the temple, in order to pass time.

Saul walked along the northern side of the temple grounds, past the Pool of Israel, past the jail and the Antonia Fortress, where it was connected to the jail, and then in a southerly direction, which was the opposite side of Solomon's Portico. He finally entered through the gate that lead him into the Court of the Gentiles, and walked east through the court until he turned the corner going again in a northerly direction and to the stairs where they normally sat on the eastern side of the temple grounds at Solomon's Portico.

When Saul arrived, he was surprised to find a fairly good sized crowd had already gathered. Some of the people he recognized and there were others which he realized had been told by the people he had left messages with earlier in the day that it was possible Jeshua would be joining them. Saul was greeted with great warmth as well as excitement, out of respect for the role that he had just played.

While the group was sitting and waiting, more people soon joined them, and small talk continued among the people. Rumors were shared and commented upon, and gossip was exchanged among the people. Not too long after the time that they would have normally began their discussions, Saul and the others could see Jeshua approaching them with three other men accompanying him.

As the four men came into hearing distance of the crowd, which now numbered over sixty people, different individuals started to shout out words of greeting to Jeshua. Jeshua smiled broadly and stopped several feet away from the first step. Saul immediately rose from his position on the fourth step, and approached Jeshua, and the two men embraced. Jeshua then separated the two of them, still holding his hands on the upper arms of Saul and looked into his eyes, and said, "Saul, it's so good to see you."

Saul's heart fluttered, as he once again felt the stirring in his soul, as the man from Galilee's look penetrated into his very being. He again was taken aback in looking at the beauty and strength in Jeshua's face. At the same time, Saul was consciously aware of the buzzing and murmur through the crowd, who had acted with surprise and admiration over the personal greeting of the two men.

Jeshua and Saul then parted, Saul taking several steps back as Jeshua then said to the crowd, "Please let me introduce my three friends. One, some of you have already met, who is Andrew, the brother of Peter. My two other friends are John and James, who have traveled with me all the way from the Sea of Galilee to be here in Jerusalem. I hope you have kind thoughts for my beloved friends."

A number of different people shouted out words of greeting to Jeshua and the three men, acknowledging Jeshua's request. Jeshua then turned to the three of them and said something in a soft voice, and as happened during the previous two visits, his followers turned and walked up the stairs to their right and took seats behind the crowd. Jeshua then turned to the group and asked, "And what shall we talk about today? What would be of interest to you for us to discuss?"

One of the men in the middle of the crowd stood up and asked, "Jeshua, what is the most important emotion or feelings that one can have? Is it dedication to the Lord, honoring our parents, generosity? What, in your opinion, would be the most important thing we should have within ourselves?" Jeshua looked at his audience, giving all of them time, for each one to consider in their own mind how they might answer this question.

Jeshua then said, "There is no more important force in the entire universe, than the life force of love that you can share with others. You should allow it to pour from yourself continuously, for all to receive. You should never restrict your flow of love for others. It should always be your primary force. Do not allow it to rise to your surface for just a few moments, and then get lost in the waves of materialism, which absorbs the lives of most people. Not enough people realize the absolute power of love, the very life force that it has in and of itself."

Jeshua continued, "I say to you, my brothers," and Jeshua looked up and noticed there were a few women sitting in the row immediately behind the last row where the men were seated on the stairs, and smiling, said "and my sisters. Be love and gentleness and all around you, you shall create the same. Love is the motivating force for the universe, for love is God. Allow the love to flow through you, and you will see its tremendous power of illumination. That power of God, through love, will transcend everything that you come in contact with you."

The crowd was totally silent, as Jeshua presented these words in a gentle yet passionate voice. A realization came to Saul that Jeshua was speaking in a slightly different tone of voice than he had when he spoke here last, many, many months before. Saul wondered if this was because Jeshua was more at ease with the familiarity of the setting and some of the people who were gathered before him, or if he was just more at ease with the words that he was sharing with them.

Another man then rose from his seat, and asked in a loud voice, "Jeshua. I know that you've touched on this before, when we met months ago, but where is God to be found? Although you have said the spirit of God resides within us, is not God in reality a separate entity that controls our lives?"

Jeshua listened carefully to the person asking the question, giving him direct eye contact. When the man had finished and sat down,

Jeshua bowed his head down, looked to the ground and slowly paced several steps to his right and then several steps to his left, then back again to his right. After about 15 seconds of silence, he raised his head and looked directly at the crowd and said, "Yes, some of you do cry out in anguish, 'Where is God? Why doesn't God intervene and stop the suffering of our young children, and stop the destruction that has taken place in the past, and yes, and even now?' You ask, 'Has God forsaken and forgotten his children? And you ask these questions, which do indeed imply that God is a separate entity, and why does he not show his willingness to control our lives, now, as perhaps He has done in the past?

"Do you not know that God has created us, his children, and God has created our playground, the world that we live within? And God has created an environment for us to be with him, that varies with the seasons, day and night, food for us to grow, produce for us to harvest and eat, and the elements that give us potential pleasure as well as pain, for our comfort, and yes, for our discomfort.

"And God said, 'It is now your world and your life. I give you the free will to live your life as you choose. But you have the ability to love each other, to create, to share and to have compassion. I have given you the intellect to reason, the physical ability to help others, the resources to create and sustain life. But God also gave us the greatest gift that He could possibly bestow upon us."

Jeshua continued, "The gift of his energy, his life, his spirit, for indeed, God does reside within each and every one of us. You are a child of God. You are part of the Oneness that we know as God. Just as the player of the harp is part of the collective musical group that he is playing with, or the person who is in political power is part of the government, or that you as an individual are part of your own society." Jeshua continued to explain the responsibility to God that each individual has, repeating some of the messages he had shared months earlier.

More questions followed, as Jeshua very carefully, with both passion and sensitivity, answered each and every one of them, sharing his profound wisdom. One of the people asked Jeshua how to handle the suffering one experiences when losing a loved one, and Jeshua answered, "For those of you who have experienced the pain of losing a child or loved one, take comfort in knowing that they are with their other parent, God, who will see that they are never in pain, or hardship while they are in his care in the other dimension. God lent you his child and God will care for your loved one until you are with your loved one again."

Saul couldn't tell how much time had gone by. He was listening so intently to every word Jeshua said that he was filled with emotion. Finally, at the completion of one of the questions that Jeshua had been asked, Jeshua looked up at his three followers and said, "Come, it's time now for us to leave," and the three descended the stairs and stood alongside him.

The crowd murmured words of tremendous thanks for having joined them and sharing his beliefs and Jeshua responded in kind. As these farewells were being said, Saul emerged from his seat and walked down the several steps and stood to the side to Jeshua's left. Finally Jeshua turned to him and walked towards him, and embraced him again.

Jeshua said, "Saul, tomorrow morning I'll be traveling to the Jordan River to visit a very dear friend. Will you meet me on the road to the Jordan River, which is next to the pinnacle of the temple shortly after sunrise? We'll travel together. Do have something to eat before we meet, for we won't be stopping for food along the way. Can you join me?"

"Of course Jeshua, of course I'll join you," Saul responded with a big smile. Saul noticed that Jeshua's three followers were standing several feet to the right hand side of Jeshua, listening to their conversation. With the exception of Andrew, who had a gentle smile on his face, the other two men, John and James were looking at Saul with no facial expression and eyes that appeared less than friendly.

Saul recognized their names as two of the men that Martha and Mary had told him were two of the fishermen brothers who were pupils of Jeshua and at times traveled with him, providing protection and security. Like the other pair of brothers, they were fishermen from the Sea of Galilee and Saul could tell from their bearing as well as their clothes, that they appeared to be simple men.

Jeshua and Saul then said their farewells. Saul watched as the four men walked from the portico to the direction of the eastern gate to leave the temple grounds. Saul would spend that evening enjoying a quiet meal at his hillside home, and then sitting outside enjoying a pleasant evening from the stone bench, overlooking the lower city. He watched the lanterns and lamps begin to be lit below. He sat in meditation and deep thought and his heart was filled with great joy as he looked forward to spending the next day with Jeshua on their journey to the Jordan River.

Chapter 16

To the Jordan River

Saul was waiting alongside the road located immediately east of the pinnacle of the temple, which would lead them to the Jordan River. He saw Jeshua and several others approaching him from a westerly direction. As they got closer, he recognized that Mary, the sister of Lazarus and Martha was also with Jeshua as well as three men. Two of the men he'd seen previously, which were the brothers John and James that were with Jeshua when he appeared at the temple the previous day.

There was a third man, who appeared to be dressed more like a native of Jerusalem, rather than one of the fishermen from Galilee. He was slightly shorter than average in height, thin, wore a loosely fitted brown tunic half way down his calves, and a turban which had

been loosely wrapped around his head. His beard was short and slightly pointed.

"Saul, thank you for joining us," Jeshua said, with a loving, friendly smile as he approached Saul and embraced him. He then stepped back, and said, "Of course you know Mary, and you met James and John yesterday. Let me introduce you to another of my friends who is from here, Jerusalem, whose name is Thomas. He has a twin brother that oddly enough, is almost as handsome as he is." His comment caused laughter among the group. Thomas glanced at Saul with a friendlier look on his face then the other companions of Jeshua had given him, stating "Saul, I'm glad to meet you."

"As I am also," Saul responded to him, as he nodded his head in acknowledgment. Saul ignored saying hello to the other two brothers, just as they also didn't greet him, but Saul turned to Mary and said "Mary, it's good to see you again. Thank you for leaving that message at the market place for me. I'm very grateful for your thoughtfulness." Mary responded with a beautiful smile on her face, "Well, Jeshua was anxious to see you also Saul, so all of us benefited."

Jeshua then turned to the group and said, "Come, let's begin our journey." They now began to walk in a westerly direction, on the road that would take them to the Jordan River. The beginning of the road that they were traveling on was wide enough for them to walk in two rows with three abreast. In the front row, Jeshua walked in the middle, with Saul on his left and Mary on his right. The three disciples walked approximately five paces behind them, also three abreast.

Saul noticed the strength and agility of Jeshua, as he took long graceful strides. It was obvious to Saul that Jeshua was used to walking in the outdoors, probably because of his regular trips between Capernaum, through Samaria, and into Judea. Often times Jeshua would shorten his stride, in order to accommodate Mary's ability to keep up with the group.

On the first portion of their trip, the terrain was relatively flat, until they got further west, outside of the city limits, and they then found themselves walking up and down gentle hills, in the direction of the Jordan River, on a trip that would take them approximately two hours. As times when the road narrowed, they would walk in single file, with Jeshua leading the way, and Mary between Jeshua and Saul.

They discussed many things, along the journey. At one point Jeshua asked Saul, "You've heard me previously speak of truth, Saul. Share with me your thoughts on truth." Saul responded, "I recognize there are some people that believe that truth is always absolute. They believe that the truth of today is also the truth of tomorrow. However, I don't believe this is accurate Jeshua. For the truth of today could be as a result of a specific period of time and circumstances in which it's found. I believe what may be one person's truth, may be false to another. Does that make sense Jeshua?"

Jeshua thought for a moment and then he looked up at the sky at a beautiful bird that was flying high above them. He watched the bird in silence for a few moments, with a loving smile on his face and then turned to Saul and responded, "People are constantly searching

for the truth, and it is right that we should do so. Some people travel far and wide in their quest for truth, and will look for truth in different places, whether it be in the Himalayas, or in temples. Eventually, they'll find that the whole truth lies within yourself, and that God resides within you. That is a revelation that all will come to at the end of their long search."

The discussion on truth continued for some time, between Saul and Jeshua. Occasionally Mary would add a remark or a comment, which was treated with equal respect by both Jeshua and Saul. At one point of their discussion, Saul asked Jeshua about becoming one with God.

"Jeshua, one day at the Temple you spoke that God resides within each of us, and you compared our journey at becoming one with God, as a person trying to climb a thousand steps of a temple. There are so many questions I have regarding this journey, such as how long does it take? Do we sometimes go downwards, rather than upwards, and is there one way to achieve it better than another? Please share with me your thoughts regarding these questions."

Jeshua slowed down his pace, indicating the importance of what he was about to share with Saul. He then stated, "While a person is trying to climb the Temple, in order to reach enlightenment by being at one with God, there will be times that they will back slide on this journey. It's even possible some people may back slide so much, that they are back again to the beginning of their ascension. If you should slide back Saul, don't feel that you have lost the ability of becoming at one with God, but rather that you are being given another opportunity to proceed forward."

Jeshua continued, "By your question, it's obvious that you're preoccupied with the completion of your journey. Don't focus on your destination Saul, but focus on the journey itself. Your arrival at your destination to be at one with God is absolute and pre-determined. You should have no doubts, no fears and no anxieties. You will arrive on schedule Saul. It cannot be otherwise. What you control is what you create on your journey to your destination."

Saul then asked, "Is there one method of being able to achieve becoming at one with God, that's better than another?" Jeshua almost came to a complete stop, slowing down his walk considerably. He turned to Saul and said, "There is no method that is preferable to another. It's all part of your life experience. It's your journey, your choice, you create it. God doesn't care whether you have to be taught truth a thousand times before you accept it. It's your choice. No two journeys are alike. In fact, it's not right for a person to assume that your choice of one path is better than another. Also it's not right to assume superiority because another person may not be at your level of enlightenment, as you become closer to being at one with God. The outcome of being at one with God is going to happen. Your personal experiences, your perception of the journey are what you create, not the outcome, which is already predestined."

Saul then asked "As you are getting closer to being at one with God, do you feel that you're a different person? I would think that you would be considerably changed." They were now walking at their normal pace and Jeshua was looking straight ahead at the horizon. He responded without looking at Saul "The higher level of awareness is he, who you are. You are not becoming someone else,

for that someone else is you. Greater understanding as you become closer to being at one with God is automatic. What is optional is the pain that you experience while you are on your journey, the disease that you may create for yourself, or your discomfort that you choose to experience along the way."

Saul then asked "How can you control sickness, or pain that's within you. I don't understand what you mean Jeshua." Jeshua responded, "Hundreds of years ago the Greeks had a word that they used called daemons. They referred to daemons as undesirable traits, emotions or attitudes, which could cause people discomfort, including disease, sickness and pain, both physically as well as possibly mentally. These daemons included such things as jealousy, anger, revenge, lack of compassion, hatred, selfishness, and other thoughts and actions and behaviors that are inconsistent with being at one with God. It was felt that not only can these daemons cause sickness and disharmony within a person, but also the person had the ability to heal himself, if they could acknowledge and forgive themselves for past behavior of these daemons so that they are no longer a part of them.

That is why I say to you Saul; you control your own journey, and the quality of the journey that you are on. There will come a time when I will help others who have already hurt themselves on their journey by having them release those daemons and teach them how to forgive themselves and also hopefully release the sickness or disease that they may be experiencing. This would not only help them to enjoy their journey better, but enable them to become enlightened faster, in becoming at one with that part of God that's

inside of them."

These words had great meaning to Saul. They walked in silence for many minutes after Jeshua shared these thoughts with him, as Saul processed them in his mind as well as in his heart. He was so grateful for Jeshua sharing his wisdom with him. Unfortunately, several hundred years in the future, the pre-medieval Roman church would choose to change the word daemons to instead being demons and try to convey to others that many people at the time that Jeshua walked the earth were possessed with evil spirits. It was part of the obsession that the future church had in trying to create fear in people, as opposed to winning their hearts and minds through love.

As the six of them continued their journey and were now on a path south of Jericho, north of Bethabara, they found themselves walking on open ground that was mostly just sand. However, it had been compacted into very hard ground, as a result of hundreds of years of people taking the same path from Jerusalem to the Jordan River, which was now only a short distance away.

As they continued on their journey westward, at one point Saul asked Jeshua "It appears to me that you don't hold the Sabbath sacred, as we're told in the temples by the priests. By that I mean, it's my understanding that you travel long distances during the Sabbath, and do other things which aren't consistent with the Sabbath being identified as a day of prayer as well as a day of rest."

Jeshua responded to Saul very matter of factly by stating, "Man was not made for the Sabbath Saul, the Sabbath was made for man. God doesn't love you any less on a day that is not the Sabbath, nor should you honor him any less regardless of which day it is. The

same is true of the temple, Saul. You can be as close to God or even closer while you're walking through the hills of Judea or through the desert as we are doing now, as you can within the temple."

Saul responded "Aren't you concerned that others may think that this shows a lack of respect to the temple, or to the priests, that you may express these thoughts to others?" Jeshua answered, "I don't show disrespect to the temple. It is those who allow animals to be sold on the temple grounds for sacrifice, in the name of God, who show disrespect. They then give these animals that have been killed on the Alter for Burnt Sacrifices to the priests as though they are honoring God, when in reality the priests accept it as food for their own personal use. This is not honoring God, Saul. This is pretending to honor God in order for the priests to receive free food."

Jeshua continued, "And for those who allow the money changers on the temple grounds who convert Roman coins to shekels in order to purchase the animals for sacrifice from the stalls and pens on the temple grounds in the Court Yard of the Gentiles, it is they who are dishonoring God by these acts. As we're walking along this wonderful land, as we see nature and beautiful small animals and birds along the way, I don't see any moneychangers along these pathways. And I don't see any of God's creatures being killed in order to feed the priests, claiming that in doing so, they are honoring God. Do you, Saul?"

Saul didn't answer Jeshua, but instead, his heart and mind was filled with joy for being able to receive the wisdom that was being shared with him by Jeshua. It was very shortly after that they were able to walk over the top of a rise and could see before them the

Jordan River. The river had a tremendous number of windings in it, which actually covered a distance of two hundred and fifty miles, although if it was measured in a straight line it would cover a distance from north to south of one hundred and thirty-five miles. The river's width varied from eighty feet to one hundred and eighty feet, depending on its location, and it was considered the most important river in the three provinces of Israel. Saul's vision took in the sights before him with excitement and great anticipation.

Chapter 17
John the Baptist

As the group of six travelers now arrived on the western shore of the Jordan River, to their right, approximately seventy-five yards downstream they could see a man standing in the water with his body exposed halfway above the waterline, although they couldn't hear his words. His arms were waving in the air as he was addressing a large number of people that were lying or sitting on the sand along the shoreline, in front of him.

Some of the people were sitting upright, listening to him, others were lying back on their elbows, and yet others were lying on their backs as if they were sleeping or sun bathing, trying to ignore the preaching antics of the man in front of them, partially submerged in the water. Who was this man with the long matted hair and beard,

his long, lean and muscular body partially covered with animal skins?

His name was John Ben Zachariah and his mother Elizabeth had given birth to him two years before Jeshua had been born. Elizabeth was the sister of Jeshua's mother, approximately fifteen years older in age than Mary. She had given birth very late in life to John, and felt that John indeed had been a gift from God both to herself as well as to her husband Zachariah, who had died while John was still an infant.

Although Elizabeth had tried very hard to have an influence on the life of John, she could see at a very early age he had an independent will. Even as a young man, his fiery and powerful personality had a mind of its own. He didn't have the mannerisms of temple priests or a gentle spiritual leader. Instead, he was a preacher of tremendous zeal and passion who seemed committed to a purpose beyond her comprehension.

While still a teenager, he left the home of his mother and began to roam in the wilds of the Judean hills as well as along the Jordan River preaching to anyone that he could find as a captive audience. It was here along the Jordan River that he found his best prospects. Many of the people would come to lie along the shore, in order to relax and to bathe in the cool waters of the river for relief from the hot Judean sun.

Others came specifically to hear the words of John, and had become devoted to his belief system, prophecies and words that he claimed represented the intentions of God. In addition to his own disciples that traveled with him, he had many followers as well as those who resented him.

Some of those who had not come to listen and see John, but rather to relax on the river, found his words of great interest, and others found them amusing. And of course, there were others that considered him a distraction, and an invasion of their privacy. Once having arrived to the shoreline of the Jordan they would all become part of his captive audience.

As the six of them approached John and the approximate seventy to eighty people that were lying along the shoreline in front of John, they stopped within twenty yards, to watch the scene that was unfolding before them, as well as to listen to his words. The three disciples stood approximately ten feet away from Jeshua, Mary and Saul, several feet further back from the three of them and observed John with great curiosity and astonishment. It had been the first time they had seen John, or had heard his words. They were taken back by the sight before them.

On the other hand, Mary maintained her beautiful dimpled smile which was a constant facial demeanor for her, while Jeshua squinted his eyes in the sunlight, and also had a slight smile on his face as he looked amused at the scene before them. Saul now stood to the right side of Jeshua, one step behind him, with both his fists resting against his hips, and a look on his face that did not disguise the astonishment that was within him.

John paused for one second, nodded in the direction of Jeshua, smiled momentarily and then turned back to his audience. "And do you think that God does not see and hear every deed that you do, as well as every sin that you commit? And do you not believe that God

will reward you for your good deeds, as well as to punish you who do sin? But even you who are the sinners, there is hope for you, for you can redeem yourself. If you are truly sorry for your sins, and want to be forgiven, come forth, and I will wash your sins away, so you may start fresh, with a clean heart and a clean soul."

John continued with his words of intimidation, speaking and shouting in a large booming voice to those who sat or lay in front of him on the sand along the river. He then pointed at a slightly heavy set young man dressed in a short dark blue tunic and shouted, "You come up here, you, right there. Are you not a sinner? Have you not committed acts in which you were embarrassed in the eyes of God for having done so? You come forward; let me wash your sins away so you can start a new life, one full of good deeds, so you may receive the awards of God. Come now for God and all others to see."

The young man looked slightly confused and embarrassed. He sat up, then placed his knee in front of him, and slowly came to a standing position and hesitantly walked toward John, into the water.

When he reached John, John put his hands on the man's shoulders and shoved him down to his knees in front of him, so the only portion of his body that was above the water was his upper chest and his head. John then shouted, "Repent, repent, and let God wash away yours sins." After he said that, John took a step backwards and putting his weight on the man's shoulders, he thrust the man forward in his direction, putting his entire face and head under the water and held him in that position for several seconds.

He then released his hands from the man, and the man raised his head, slightly choking from water which had gone into his mouth unexpectedly from the sudden thrust into the river, and he spit out droplets of water from his mouth. The three disciples standing to the right of Jeshua, Mary and Saul were trying to contain themselves from laughter and shook their heads in disbelief. Saul looked at Jeshua, and he had a smile and a bemused look on his face, as he continued to watch the scene unfold.

John continued to preach and shout at his audience until approximately half the people, one at a time, finally approached John in the water, and allowed themselves to be immersed, although John was gentler with the rest then he had been with the first man. After approximately an hour had gone by, John finally stopped his preaching. Recognizing that no others were willing to step forward to also be dunked into the river, John stopped speaking and stared at his audience for about half a minute. He then turned to Jeshua, without saying a word, opening both of his arms in his direction as if welcoming Jeshua to join him.

Jeshua began wading into the river and when he had almost reached John, John shouted out toward the group, "I am here, I am here to show you the way. And this beloved man before me, he is the way." Jeshua now stood in front of John, and very gently placed his hands on John's shoulders. He then said in a soft voice but one that could still be heard by the crowd, "John you are a messenger of God. May God bless you and your work."

Having said that, Jeshua now gently applied pressure to John's shoulders, so that he came down to his knees so that also only his upper chest and head was above the water. Then gently Jeshua laid John back in a direction away from Jeshua, until his head and face

were immersed under the water for several seconds. Then Jeshua raised John back towards him again, and then placed his hands under his armpits and lifted him to an upright position.

Jeshua then said something in a voice so soft that the crowd that sat behind Jeshua, as well as the five members of his traveling party could not hear his words. When he was finished, he and John embraced each other, and then Jeshua turned and waded out of the water back in the direction of Saul, Mary and his three disciples. When he reached them, he gently said, "Come, it is time for us to go," and all six of them turned and began walking back in the direction that they had come.

Saul and Jeshua discussed many things during the approximate two-hour trip to arrive back to the place they had started, north of the temple, near the Pool of Bethsaida. Saul had many questions that he asked Jeshua, that Jeshua patiently answered. Mary also listened very intently and would also occasionally ask Jeshua a question as well as Saul.

Saul had asked Jeshua when he would be traveling again to Jerusalem, so he could spend more time with him. Jeshua answered "Saul, I am like a shepherd with many sheep. I can't tell you exactly when I'll be back, but please understand there will be times when I will be back in the Judea area but won't be able to visit with you. Please don't take it personally, for I have come to love you very much and consider you a dear friend. We will spend time together, but do know that you will constantly be in my thoughts and in my heart and we will see each other when the occasions are right. But never lose sight that you are on a journey and I will always be with you in thought and spirit, even when we are not together physically."

Although Saul was disappointed he wouldn't be able to see Jeshua as often as he wanted to, he understood his words and found great comfort with what Jeshua said to him, for Jeshua would also be in his thoughts. When it came time to say good-bye to each other, Mary said to Saul "Please don't be a stranger. You know where we live in Bethany, and you're always welcome at our home." Saul responded "Thank you for your kindness. I'm sure that we will see each other every so often, and please give my regards to your sister, as well to your brother."

He then turned to the three disciples who were standing behind Jeshua to Saul's left. John and James stared expressionlessly at Saul, although not with the same hostility that the other disciple, Peter had shown. He still couldn't see any signs of friendship on their faces. Thomas, however, the follower of Jeshua from Jerusalem that he had just met that day, did slightly smile at Saul and say "Good bye Saul."

Saul responded to his salutation, and Saul directed it to all three of them and then looked at Jeshua once more, and the two men embraced. They were almost exactly the same height, taller than the average man, but a contrast in looks. Jeshua's long silken brown hair fell to his shoulders, with highlights of gold from the sun, in contrast to Paul's shorter black hair, curled and in waves. Jeshua's beard was also longer than Saul's, each being the color of their hair.

Jeshua's blue gray eyes were filled with love, kindness and wisdom as he looked into Saul's eyes which were also filled with love as well as gratitude. The two men smiled at each other, without saying another word. Saul then turned and began walking in a

southerly direction towards the temple and lower city, while Jeshua, Mary and the three disciples began walking again in a southeast direction in order to connect to the road to Bethany. Much time would go by before Saul would see Jeshua again.

Chapter 18
The Passing of Time

As the years went by, for Saul life would continue on the same path he had been on since traveling to the Jordan River with Jeshua. In Jerusalem the citizens continued to feel the pressure of the tax burdens imposed on them. Although Saul didn't resent the occupation of the Romans in Judea, and since he had been raised as a child in a part of the world that had been under Roman occupation, he basically accepted that as a fact of life.

However, he did feel a great deal of sympathy and compassion for the people he came in contact with in Jerusalem, who had difficulty in meeting the burden of paying taxes not only to those who were responsible domestically for the governing of Israel, but also the tribute which they were required to pay to the Romans.

Other parts of the Roman Empire benefited tremendously from Roman occupation. Some of these countries had been at civil war internally, or were involved in costly fighting with organized groups of bandits and warlords who took it upon themselves to exhort money from its citizens as well as plunder their properties and riches. Many of the countries had suffered economically because of the fear of the traders that gangs and robbers would attack them while they were traveling either to import or export goods to the local people, and were reluctant to visit those places that were unsafe. With Roman occupation, they ended any civil wars that were taking place within those countries, as well as put the robbers and the brigands out of business.

In many cases, these small countries did not have armies, so that the occupation of the Romans took place without the loss of lives or properties. Not only did the Romans introduce their culture, but their tremendous engineering skills could be seen in the construction of new roads and highways, which substantially increased the trade of importing and exporting into those regions that previously were not receiving the benefit of this commerce. The Romans also built aqueducts, sanitation systems, and provided other amenities, which previously were not available to these areas.

Saul understood all of this, and didn't feel a country becoming part of the Roman Empire necessarily a negative. On the other hand, there was a direct relationship between the benevolence or the lack of it by those Romans who were placed in power over the local communities, which could be devastating if those in leadership were cruel and indifferent to the needs of the local people. Unfortunately,

Jerusalem had been exposed to their share of incompetent and cruel Roman leaders who had been put in positions of power, who demanded the allegiance and loyalty of the local citizens.

It had only been a short period of time ago, that a new Procurator had been appointed, whose name was Pontius Pilate. Pilate was a person who had risen to a position of power and authority in Rome, after having accumulated substantial wealth and having become close to the emperor Tiberius. He had very quickly developed a reputation in Jerusalem of being a person who was not only cruel, but who was also deceitful. His lack of respect and arrogance to the local population only added to the difficulties that the people of Jerusalem were experiencing.

Also, regarding King Herod and his heirs, the people in the provinces of Israel would many times find themselves the victims of those who were in power from the royal family within their own province. The patriarch Kind Herod had died when Saul was a still a young boy living in Tarsus. He had not only been a cruel individual, but many people believed that he was insane. Upon his death, his sons took over the ruling of the provinces of Judea, Samaria and Galilee. One of his sons also known as King Herod, was particularly disliked by the population, and was a financial burden to the citizens under his reign, which added to their financial woes of paying annual taxes to the Romans.

But nonetheless, Saul prospered tremendously over the five years since the time that he had visited the Jordan River with Jeshua, and had witnessed John preaching to the people along the Jordan. He not only was now the owner of seven stalls at the market place, but he

had also become active in the ownership of commercial land. Saul would purchase large fields of property, again paying the seller over a period of time, and would subdivide the land into smaller parcels, which he would then lease to individuals who wished to farm the land but who didn't have the financial capability themselves to purchase land for their private ownership.

Whether the tenants who were leasing his land were using the property for cultivation of olive groves or figs, for the trowing of grapes to create wine, or for other farm produce, in each case their payments to Saul exceeded the payments that he in turn had to make to the original sellers of the land. These activities continued to make Saul more and more financially independent. In fact, Saul had actually entered into some business transactions with various individuals that had caused him to expand some of his commercial activities into the city of Damascus, in the country of Syria.

In the meantime, Saul's relationship with his friend Aaron, his robust best friend with the round face, round beard and round wife Zelda, continued to grow. He not only admired Aaron's sense of humor, but found many times he could share his thoughts with Aaron, and receive responses that were both intelligent and thought provoking. A portion of his social life surrounded his friendship with Aaron and Zelda, as well as his friends Talah, Shelah and Nadob.

Talah had finally settled down, in spite of his reputation as a womanizer and had married a young lady who shared with him his need to wear clothing of the highest quality and flashy jewelry and, who also gave importance to personal appearance. Saul was amused in noticing that Talah had married a woman in his same image, and indeed there were times when Talah's wife would introduce Saul to girlfriends of hers, and Saul would enjoy their company over the years.

As for Shelah, even as he matured in age, he still loved to play the role of the comedian. He was always able to find the light side of any subject, and kept Saul entertained with his outrageous remarks. Saul continued to enjoy his company over mid-morning meals at the bazaar, along with Shelah's good friend Nadob, who also still remained the perennial cynic. They were such a contrast in personalities that Saul found it particularly interesting when he is able to place both of them in the same social situation, and encourage the two of them to engage in a conversation or topics in which he knew they would be in total disagreement.

Conversely so, Saul's friends saw Saul mature not only as a person of prominence in the commercial world, but also one of substantial wisdom, intelligence and influence. Certainly, the many meetings and discussions that he had with Jeshua, not only prior to their visit together to the Jordan River, but in the years to follow, had made a major impression and influence on the life of Saul. Saul had become a total believer in Jeshua's teachings and although he could not be classified as a disciple of Jeshua, he indeed had accepted Jeshua as his teacher, and had recognized the tremendous impact that Jeshua had on his life.

The other factor that played an important role in Saul's life was his undying love for Leah. Even as the years went by, Saul had never been able to release the affection and love he felt inside, as if it were cemented into his heart. Even though he had met many of the most

attractive and exciting young women in Jerusalem, some who had temporarily become his lady friends, there was no room within his being that enabled him to feel any special affection or love for these temporary flings.

It wasn't because he hadn't tried. Several times he had thrown himself head first into a relationship, hoping that the companionship of his new lady friend and the chemistry that is found between new lovers, would release him from that constant ache within his heart. He tried very hard to let go of the anguish and pain over the love that was inside him, like a permanent affliction. He never made false promises to his lady friends, nor ever gave them false hopes.

Although he didn't share with them that there was another woman in his heart, he did let them know they should not take their relationship seriously, for he had no intentions of marriage. Because of this, when his newest lady friend would recognize that he indeed was serious regarding his lack of intentions, the relationship would soon be over. It was the norm in Jerusalem for eligible women to be married in their late teens and they didn't want to waste valuable time with a person, no matter how attractive or how wealthy, who was committed to not taking the relationship seriously.

It was not difficult for him to end the companionship of any of these ladies. With Leah, his choice of not marrying was one that he himself didn't fully understand other than he knew that marriage was not his mission in life. He knew that he had to have the independence and freedom from marriage and children, although he really didn't know why.

At times he did wonder if this was a carry-over from the

dysfunctional marriage of his own mother and father that he had witnessed as a child, and other times he felt there was some other reason much more significant than his childhood experiences. His having released Leah was not because of the issue of marriage, for he would have continued seeing her for the rest of his life, had she chose to. But it was out of his deep love for Leah that he released her so that she could move on to a life of her own and have the loving husband and family that she deserved. In his new relationships, he didn't feel that he was sacrificing or losing anything as they dissipated, since he felt no love for these women and his interest was only to enjoy their company on a temporary basis.

He did see Leah from time to time, always in a public situation so their feelings could be treated platonically. The last meeting they had took place in a quiet restaurant in the bazaar, underneath the awnings of an establishment specializing in Egyptian food and wine. At this meeting, Leah shared with Saul that she intended to move on with her life and had truly given up any hope of their being together.

Leah said, "Saul, I am now 23 years old, and it has been five years since that night that we had dinner with Aaron and Zelda, and we said goodbye to one another as sweethearts and lovers." Leah looked down at the table and began playing with several crumbs, her fingers lightly moving them around in circles. With her eyes sad and downcast, beginning to fill with tears, she continued, "I recognized that I must move on with my life, for I don't want to find myself one day as an elderly spinster without any children to share my life and no grandchildren sitting on my lap. There is a man that I have been seeing for over a year now who has asked me to marry him. I have

accepted his proposal. I will always be a faithful wife and hopefully a loving mother to the children that we'll have. But no matter how many years go by, I know that I will always have your love in my heart and shall always pray for your good health and happiness."

Saul felt a rush of mixed emotions. One part of him ached inside, realizing that some other man would have Leah as his wife and the mother of the children that could have been his. At the same time, he felt an emotion pass through him, almost the release of guilt because Leah was now going to move on with her life as she should, rather than her suffering loneliness as a spinster because of the love they had for each other and had shared at one time in the past.

Saul finally responded in a quiet voice, "Leah, I will also always love you. There will never be another woman in my life that will replace you. But I will never say this to you again, for I don't want to affect the happiness that you're entitled to and that I hope you'll find in the marriage you're committing to."

In an effort to change the sadness of the situation, Saul then said with laughter in his voice, "And please do not name any of your sons Saul."Leah laughingly responded, "Oh, don't worry! That I shall not do! You can be absolutely assured of that." After a few more moments of silence, they both realized it was time to part and not carry on any further conversation.

They both stood up and embraced each other for what seemed like an eternity, both grateful that they had been seated in the rear of the restaurant, out of sight of most of the other diners. As they held each other in that last embrace, Leah began to sob in his arms and tears were flowing down Saul's cheeks. They parted at the same time, holding each other at arm's length as they gazed into each other's eyes. Quietly Saul said, "Goodbye my love." "Goodbye my love," Leah answered. They then turned their backs to each other and went their separate ways. It would be many years before they would see each other again.

Chapter 19

Journey to Capernaum

Although Saul did not see Jeshua as often as he wished over that five year period, he still made every effort to spend every moment with Jeshua that Jeshua was able to provide to him. During one of Jeshua's visits, he invited Saul to travel with him from Jerusalem to Capernaum, so he would get a better opportunity to see firsthand the life Jeshua was leading outside of his visits to Saul's beloved and adopted city of Jerusalem.

When they began their trip out of Jerusalem, Saul recognized that the number of pupils who had attached themselves to Jeshua had grown in number. There were now seven individuals that he could identify as fishermen, having come from towns along the western shore of the Sea of Galilee. Two of them were Peter who Jeshua sometimes called Cepheus, and his brother Andrew, who were both

from Bethsaida. Andrew was a quiet individual, but he noted Peter along with John ben Zebedee had become more vocal as years had gone by.

The other set of brothers, John and James, who were the sons of Zebedee, were also constantly with Jeshua, in his travels. It appeared to Saul that both Peter and John had emerged as leaders among the disciples, who constantly seemed to be vying with one another to have a closer relationship with Jeshua. Three of the other followers that Jeshua had come to recognize on a constant basis, who were also from Galilee, were Philip, Thaddeus and Bartholomew. Bartholomew was the most outspoken of the three, but they were relatively quiet, as compared to Peter and John.

There were also several more individuals who were from Jerusalem, who attended to Jeshua's needs when he was in Jerusalem, who were part of the group of disciples. In addition to Thomas there was Matthew, who worked in Jerusalem as a tax collector, as well as another James, Simon and Judas. Saul didn't see this last group of individuals as often as he would see the Galileans with Jeshua, for obviously they had their own lives, homes and families to attend to, even when Jeshua was visiting Jerusalem.

Regarding all of these disciples, in reality, Saul recognized that none of them were friendly toward him. He could often feel their indifference, and yes, even in some cases, their hostility toward him, for they couldn't identify with Saul any more than he could identify with them. He assumed that they resented his wealth, his lifestyle, the fact that he had a substantial formal education as compared to theirs, and most importantly they resented the fact that his relationship with Jeshua was on a one-on-one basis, while theirs was a group relationship.

Conversely so, the disciples of Jeshua were people of very modest income, although John and James' father Zebedee did own a fleet of fishing boats. Most of them were also family men, particularly the fishermen from Galilee, who were willing to sacrifice their relationships with their own families in order to follow Jeshua. It was not a coincidence that they didn't include Saul when they shared their stories of the life of Jeshua in their future testimonials, considering they didn't accept him as one of them, which indeed he was not.

Because Saul was not included in their testimonials which some day would be called the New Testament, most future historians would assume that Saul and Jeshua didn't know each other at the time that Saul lived in Jerusalem where Jeshua had been a constant visitor.

When Saul accompanied Jeshua from Jerusalem to Capernaum, at each town and village Saul would pay for a room at either an inn, or in a boarding house, as opposed to spending the evening with Jeshua's disciples. They in turn had already procured places to stay for themselves and Jeshua, prior to their arrival to the various towns, or if the weather conditions permitted, they would sleep outdoors in a safe park.

They would have already made arrangements before hand, in which food would be provided to them by some of the people that lived locally within each town and village, who had already become acquainted with the teachings of Jeshua, and had also been

influenced by his wonderful messages. Saul would witness Jeshua generally speaking at either a temple in some of the larger towns that they visited, or his disciples would encourage people to join them at a central location in town, such as at the town well, where Jeshua would then speak to the group that had formed.

At times Saul would feel very badly for Jeshua if the crowds were not large, and Jeshua had to share his words in front of groups as small as perhaps six or seven individuals. Others might walk by, and shake their head in disapproval, showing a lack of respect for Jeshua and his words. Saul would feel resentment and anger toward those people and felt almost a compulsion to shout at them, "Do you not know who he is? Do you not know the words that he speaks are the words of God? Why are you not sitting humbly at his feet, as he is trying to help you understand your relationship with God, and to try to teach you to become at one with that part of God that is inside of you?"

But Saul never did speak up to these people that he felt were not showing the proper respect. And although Jeshua never said a word to him and never criticized or found fault with those who were not accepting his words or giving his presence the proper attention, sometimes Saul could see a sadness in Jeshua's eyes, as well as disappointment.

The journey north from Jerusalem to Capernaum took them through many towns and villages that Saul had never previously visited. From Jerusalem they first went due west to Kirjath Jearim, and then north to Emmaus. From there they continued almost due north to Lydda, and then slightly northeast to Arimathea. They then traveled through the passes of the hills of Mt. Geriziny, into the towns of Sychar and then northwest into the heart of the province of Samaria. From there, they then continued due north to Esdraelon, and then further north into the villages of Nain and Nazareth, the town where Jeshua's family originally lived before he was born.

Saul noticed a tremendous difference between these people living in these rural areas north of the metropolis of Jerusalem. Their temples were very small and unostentatious, and a larger percentage of the population were pagans, as opposed to the small number of non-Jews that were living in Jerusalem and the Judean province. Those who were not of the Jewish faith were called Gentiles, which meant that they were not of the Judaic faith. And some of the Gentiles were pagans, in that they prayed to false gods such as wooden idols and statues, which the Jews often jokingly referred to as praying to lemon trees. Those who had no belief system what-so-ever were referred to simply as Gentiles.

Saul found these people to be more casual and relaxed than the people in Jerusalem whose lives were much more complicated and under stress. But at the same time, he also recognized that they were much less religious, and they didn't have the intense interest in hearing the words of Jeshua, as those people that he had witnessed listening to the wisdom of Jeshua in Jerusalem.

From Nazareth, they then traveled due north to Cana, then from Cana, due east to Tiberius and the Sea of Galilee. Now they were among people that were friends and family of the disciples, and Saul had a great deal of interest in the lives of the people that lived along the shores of the Sea of Galilee.

He noticed that the land in Tiberius and north into Magdala, as they were getting closer to Capernaum, enjoyed lush rolling hills, with vegetation and farm produce growing in great abundance. He learned that the Sea of Galilee was a major source of commerce in which the fish were caught not only for local consumption, but also sent down in great quantities to Jerusalem to be purchased, cooked and sold by the local population in that metropolis. Also, a tremendous amount of the produce that was grown in the hillsides along the Sea of Galilee would find its way also into Jerusalem.

As a result of this commerce, he found the towns along the Sea of Galilee much more exciting and bustling with activity, then the small villages and towns that he had encountered traveling with Jeshua and the disciples going north from Jerusalem. There was much more of a heterogeneous group of people of different nationalities. Saul enjoyed watching the excitement and activities along the docks where the fishermen actively worked, as well as within the heart of the towns, where travelers purchased goods to transport south into Jerusalem, as well as the local population doing their shopping and bargaining.

Those sights brought back memories to Saul of the first few months that he had lived in the Holy Land, when he first settled in Caesarea and saw the same type of activities. Saul was particularly looking forward to the last leg of this journey, where he would meet the other members of the family of Jeshua.

The night before they went into Capernaum, they rested in Magdala. Saul found himself staying at a home of one of the local people, a short distance from the Sea of Galilee. The house was perched on a hillside, which provided Saul an opportunity to enjoy the view overlooking the lake and the activities on its shoreline. Saul was told that the population within Capernaum was actually as large as thirty-five thousand people, which surprised him. He learned that Capernaum was the major port that was used commercially on this body of water.

The house in Magdala was quite large and the accommodations had been arranged for not only him, as well as a number of the disciples who did not live in Magdala and didn't have relatives in that town. That evening Saul made an effort to try to talk to some of the disciples, but found they were not willing to show any friendship towards him. The one person that he was able to engage in conversation on fairly regular basis, who seemed more indifferent to Saul, rather than unfriendly, was Thomas, who lived in Jerusalem, but was originally from Cyrene.

Saul invited Thomas to walk with him along the shoreline after supper, and Thomas agreed. There was a substantial breeze blowing across the lake and both men had placed their hoods over their heads, and tied them under their chin for warmth and comfort. Saul was considerably taller and broader then Thomas, and they walked at a very slow pace as they trudged along the shoreline in a northerly direction.

"Have you been to Capernaum before?" asked Saul. "Yes, many times. I'm not a stranger there." answered Thomas. Saul then asked, "Share with me Thomas, what do you and your friends think of Jeshua, and the messages that he shares with you?" Thomas looked down at his feet as he continued walking seeming to search for the

right answer, after a few seconds he finally said, "There are many times when I feel that my friends, as you call them, do not understand what he is saying.

"Often times he will give them examples, an analogy, in order to try to make them understand things on a simpler basis, but Saul, the fact that they don't have the education, and may not be as bright as you, doesn't mean that they're not good people. They are good men, and they are loyal and respect Jeshua, even if they don't totally understand him."

Saul responded, "I didn't imply that they were not good people Thomas. I was just curious as to whether or not they are aware of what a special relationship this man has with God. I am sure that it must have crossed your mind more than once, that Jeshua might actually be the Messiah, as has been prophesied in the holy books."

Again, Thomas looked down at the ground, as if he was thinking and trying to choose his words carefully. He responded, "We have discussed that among ourselves. We're not sure but we recognize that it may be possible that Jeshua is indeed the Messiah that has been prophesied would come." Thomas hesitated and then added, "Why do you continue with your relationship with him Saul? Who do you think he is?"

Saul looked at Thomas and answered without hesitation, "I think he has more wisdom then any person that I've met before in my life. I feel he has a much greater understanding of our relationship with God, and how we're supposed to manifest God in our lives. As to whether or not he is the Messiah, I certainly believe that it's possible. I remember a time when I asked him if he was the son of

God, and he answered me "Saul, do you not know, we are all God's children, and he then laughed that beautiful, wonderful laugh that he has."

Thomas didn't respond to Saul's answer, instead they continued to walk in silence. Finally after several minutes, Saul then asked Thomas, "What's his family like? Surely you must have met them."Thomas responded, "Yes, I have met them a number of times. You know that his father passed away when Jeshua was about 16 years old. His mother Mary is a beautiful woman. Her heart is full of sweetness, and she only knows kindness and compassion. She sees everything and keeps a lot of her thoughts to herself, but you can see the great love and devotion that she has for Jeshua." Saul then asked, "And the rest of his family, tell me of his brothers and sisters."

Thomas again thought carefully before answering and then said, "The next oldest is his brother James, who is seven years younger than Jeshua. They are nothing alike. James resents that Jeshua travels so much and doesn't have a regular job as others do. James feels that he's wasting his time and is an embarrassment to the family as he goes around different parts of Israel, teaching as he does.

"The next oldest is his sister Ruth, who has a great deal of love for Jeshua. She has total devotion to Jeshua and would follow him if she were not a woman. As for the youngest brother, whose name is Jude, he's a person of simple tastes, who smiles a lot and doesn't take too many things seriously. I doubt if he has a serious opinion as to whether Jeshua should be preaching or not, or whether he should stay in Capernaum and work and live, as does James."

Saul then said with tremendous sincerity, "Thomas, I don't see Jeshua as often as you. There are times when many, many months go by between our visits. Would you mind if I could see you every so often while in Jerusalem, in order for you to share with me what may be happening in Jeshua's life at different times?" Thomas looked up at Saul and seemed somewhat surprised, that Saul would ask that.

Although Thomas didn't have feelings of friendship towards Saul, he respected him and he was aware of his commercial success as well as his education and intelligence. He was actually flattered that Saul would make this request. He answered, "That's not a problem. Please feel free to call upon me whenever you choose. I live in the lower city, just about three streets east of the market place". Thomas continued to give him directions as to how to find the house, as they walked slowly up the hill back to their lodgings.

When they arrived at the house, Saul thanked Thomas for taking the time to walk with him along the lake, as well as answering his questions. They then said good night and Saul proceeded to the small bedroom in the loft area that had been assigned to him. He slept well that night, and his last thoughts were filled with anticipation of their visit to Capernaum that would take place in the morning.

Chapter 20

Capernaum

The following morning Saul joined a group of people for breakfast including some of the disciples. They ate in the big eating area next to the kitchen in the house in which they were staying. The main course included large plates filled with salted fish, in addition to cucumbers that had been soaked in vinegar and assorted fresh fruits. Saul hadn't yet seen Jeshua that morning. He assumed that he had either eaten earlier, or was enjoying breakfast at a different location.

Approximately a half an hour after the meal was completed, the traveling group gathered their sacks containing their personal belongings, and slung them over their shoulders. They then began to assemble outside of the house to begin the journey from Magdala to

Capernaum. They estimated it would probably take between two and two and a half hours, depending on how fast they walked.

When the group left the house it consisted of over twenty people. Jeshua was walking in the front with several others. Saul intentionally stayed towards the middle of the pack, for he realized that he was a guest and didn't want to impose himself into a position he was not entitled to. He knew that many of these people had known Jeshua for many years, prior to Saul having met him. Saul also noticed that Peter and John were walking towards the rear, and he made a point of wanting to walk along side of them, hoping to bridge the gap of the unfriendliness that existed between him and them.

As they walked along a well traveled dirt road between Magdala and Capernaum, the sun had risen high enough over the eastern hills, so that it was reflecting on the beautiful lake that was below their view from the road to their right. The reflections of sunlight sparkled off of the multi-colored sails of the pleasure boats and of the discolored faded white sails of the fishing vessels. Even though it was early in the morning, there was a substantial amount of activity along the shoreline as the fishermen were assembling their equipment in preparation for going out to seek their daily catches.

Fifteen minutes into the walk, Saul noticed the group was made up of not only some of the disciples that lived along the Sea of Galilee, but also members of their families that wanted to spend as much time as possible with them, since they'd been away for the last several months. Saul intentionally slowed down his pace so Peter would catch up with him who was now walking to his immediate left.

Saul glanced at Peter and said "I understand you're from Bethsaida, which is quite north of here. Is Bethsaida similar to what we've seen in Tiberius and Magdala?" Peter looked at Saul with a frown on his face, recognizing that Saul was trying to engage him in small talk, and wanting to show his lack of enthusiasm, he answered, "No, it isn't. Bethsaida is smaller and different."

Saul realized that he better make an effort to talk about something of greater substance, or he wouldn't accomplish his purpose. He then commented "It must be difficult for you to be away from your family while you're traveling. I'm not married so I don't have a family, but I know there must be hardships to be separated from your wife. And I understand that you have two children."

Peter didn't answer at first, and Saul thought perhaps he wouldn't, since he really didn't ask him a question. But after twenty seconds of silence had gone by, Peter said "It's not hard to make sacrifices, when there is good reason behind it. I have no regrets for spending the time with Jeshua, for being with him and helping him has become my first priority."

Saul considered whether he should comment on Peter's response, but before he could answer Peter then said "But you don't have that problem, do you? Your business activities are your family, and they would be more important to you then caring for Jeshua, wouldn't they be?"

Saul tried to make eye contact with Peter as he answered "I've never tried to compare the two. There's nothing I can offer Jeshua as he travels outside of Jerusalem. I've watched how you and the other

disciples care for his needs, and there's nothing I can do for him that is not already being done better than I could provide."

Peter continued to look straight ahead, and then in a lower voice, as though his defenses were softened, he stated, "Yes, that's probably true. Perhaps someday Jeshua's needs will change, and you may find ways to provide him greater assistance. We shall see what God has in store for all of us." Saul was surprised at Peter's remark.

He thought, after his conversation with Thomas the previous night, and now from the remarks of Peter, that he may have misjudged these people somewhat. Since his contact in the past had always been with people who were more like himself regarding their education, their social lives and their commercial activities, he thought that he may have given less credit than was due to Jeshua's disciples.

Saul noticed John Ben Zebedee, the brother of James, walking several feet in front of him to his right. After he continued his walk along the side of Peter awhile longer, he quickened his pace so that he was soon walking along the left hand side of John. John glanced at Saul when he reached him and Saul said, "Hello John."

John brought up his left forearm and playfully shoved Saul, which caused Saul to break stride for a moment. "You city people don't know how to walk along the roads like us small town people," John remarked as he looked at Saul with an exaggerated expression of amusement. Saul responded, "Yes, but I'm told you fishermen have trouble staying on a camel and you ride a donkey rather than a horse, because your frightened of the speed." Both men laughed and John again bent his left arm and pushed it against Saul, knocking him slightly off balance.

The two men then engaged in small talk, which they had never done before. Saul thought that perhaps some of the barrier that previously existed between the disciples and himself may have been partially relieved on this trip. They'd been able to see the amount of respect that Saul had for Jeshua and that he didn't try to interfere or impose on their own relationship and the time they spent with Jeshua.

Saul wondered to himself if perhaps they had thought that he considered himself an equal to Jeshua, but now realized that Saul in his own way was also a pupil, even if it was on a different level than their relationship with Jeshua and therefore they were willing to hold him in less contempt then they previously did.

As they got closer to their destination approaching the outskirts of Capernaum, the group began to get excited. When they reached the outskirts of the town, there was a group of people waiting for them and formal greetings began to be shouted back and forth from the two groups as they approached one another.

Saul remained in the background, since obviously he didn't know any of the people waiting for them in Capernaum and he watched as hugs and greetings were exchanged between the people. He particularly noticed a very attractive petite lady who had hugged Jeshua, and they were now holding each other's hands and looking into each other's eyes. She was a very beautiful woman.

Saul guessed that she was probably older than she looked, and that she was most likely Jeshua's mother, Mary. Finally, after completing their greetings the group all marched together further

into the town. They took a left turn at a road that went further back away from the lake, until they came to a house which appeared to be where Mary and her family lived.

Saul continued to watch as some of the group then said good bye to Jeshua, and then went in opposite directions either to their own homes or to the homes of people that they've been assigned to stay with. Saul again didn't want to intrude on Jeshua and the people that were surrounding him, so he waited in the background until he caught Jeshua's eye.

Jeshua then motioned to Saul to come join them, which Saul did. People parted the way and allowed Saul to enter in the center of the group where Jeshua was still standing there, next to his mother and several other people. "Saul, I would like to introduce you to my family. This beautiful lady is my mother, whom is very dear to me." Jeshua then turned to Mary and said "And this is my friend Saul, who lives in Jerusalem, but he's originally from Tarsus. I should also add, he owns half the city of Jerusalem," Jeshua finished with laughter in his voice.

Mary then said "I hope Saul, it's the better half." Saul responded "I don't quite own half, but in either case, I would take any half." After some additional casual remarks, and teasing one another, Mary then said "Saul, may we offer you a seat at our table for lunch? Please do join us."

Jeshua didn't say a word, leaving the invitation to Mary and the acceptance or decline to Saul. Saul had planned to leave that afternoon to head back to Jerusalem, that same day. He was sensitive to staying over and imposing on the time that Jeshua was going to spend with his own family. He decided quickly in his mind that he could secure a horse from the rental company and easily make it to Nain before nightfall by bypassing Nazareth. So Saul answered "I'd be pleased to join you for lunch."

After they relaxed for awhile, they washed their hands and faces, drawing water from a well a short distance from them. They then entered into the house to enjoy their meal. Saul noticed that although there was not a substantial amount of furniture, the house was extremely neat and orderly, and almost all the furniture had been made out of lemonwood or cedar with exceptional workmanship.

Saul guessed that some of the furniture had been made by Jeshua's father Joseph, who had been an accomplished carpenter, and upon meeting Jeshua's younger brother Jude, he also learned that he had continued in his father's trade. As Thomas had described to Saul, Jude appeared very easy going, and a person without a tremendous amount of curiosity. He had a pleasant smile on his face, innocent looking light blue eyes, and his hair was very curly and blondish brown, as was his short beard. He was not quite as tall as Jeshua and he was huskier, and Saul could see no resemblance in either their looks or their personality.

Saul also met Jude's older brother, James, who was approximately seven years younger than Jeshua. James was very thin and aesthetic looking, with straight black hair and a pointed beard. His narrow dark eyes showed greater intelligence than Jude and he seemed to be studying not only Saul as a newcomer, but also Jeshua. He wasn't unfriendly, but neither did he volunteer any words that could be interpreted as wanting to carry on a conversation, other than

his responding to remarks.

Of Jeshua's siblings, the one who impressed him most was his sister Ruth, who was younger than James but older than Jude. She was slightly taller than her mother Mary, and slightly more stout considering Mary was so petite. She did have the resemblance of Mary's features. Saul observed that her feelings towards Jeshua were full of love and affection. It became obvious to Saul that Ruth idolized her brother Jeshua and thought the world of him.

In addition to Mary and Ruth preparing and serving the food, there was also an older woman by the name of Josie, who seemed to be part of the household. Saul gathered from the conversations taking place, that she'd been a nanny for the children while they were growing up, and had continued to live with the family ever since, as though she was a relative. But the one that impressed Saul most, not withstanding Jeshua, was his mother Mary. She listened carefully to the words of others as if each word was of great importance when they spoke. It was always with utmost respect and always with kindness and sensitivity.

Jeshua sat at the head of the table and Saul was invited the honor of sitting to Jeshua's immediate right. Saul listened to the conversations and chose only to participate when he was specifically asked a question. Again, he didn't want to intrude on this gathering of family and old friends. In addition to Jeshua's immediate family, there were several other people seated and it was obvious to Saul that they had been very close to the family for many years.

Jeshua seemed in a great mood, as he engaged in lively conversation with his family and the family friends. His conversation

The Commitment

didn't involve spirituality or the messages that he discussed when he was teaching his pupils or preaching to his large audiences in Jerusalem or as they traveled throughout Israel on their recent trip. Instead, he listened carefully to the words of others, asked questions with a genuine interest and answered any questions they had of him.

At one point, Jeshua began to tell the group a story regarding an Arab nomad. As the story went on, it was an extremely interesting and very funny anecdote that caused a great deal of laughter. Saul was particularly amused, and was laughing so hard, tears were coming to his eyes. When Jeshua had finished the story, the entire group was embraced in great laughter including Jeshua.

Saul was so filled with emotion that he took his left hand and put it on Jeshua's right forearm, and he felt filled with an intense love greater than he had ever felt before in his life. As he looked at Jeshua, whose shoulders and head was drawn back still laughing in appreciation of the story, he was overwhelmed with the love and affection he felt for this man, as well as the appreciation for his wonderful sense of humor.

When the meal was over, Saul then personally thanked those who had prepared and served the food, and told them that he would be on his way. He then went over to Jeshua, and Jeshua accompanied Saul outside. They walked together towards the road in front of the house, with Saul's sack with his personal items slung over his shoulder.

"Jeshua, thank you for letting me join you on this trip. I'm grateful for the invitation and I'm so glad that I was able to go."

"Saul, I plan to spend a considerable amount of time in Galilee, so we may not see each other for awhile, my friend. When I do come

183

back to Jerusalem, be assured I'll get notice to you so that we can spend some time together." Jeshua then looked into Saul's eyes and as always, Saul felt as if musical chords in his soul were being played. He looked into Jeshua's eyes, and saw a cloud of seriousness and almost sadness in them. "Saul, many things will happen in the future which will call for dramatic changes in my life, and even perhaps yours. Our friendship is not by accident. There are no coincidences in life, Saul. There is a purpose for our relationship."

Jeshua continued "Someday that purpose will show itself. Until then, know that I love you and you are in my thoughts. May God bless you as you continue on your journey." Saul felt tears form in his eyes, even though he wasn't sure why. He knew that he was reacting to the words of Jeshua, and the sadness that he could see in the blue gray eyes of Jeshua. Jeshua then smiled his beautiful smile at Saul and they embraced each other for a long time.

Without saying another word, Saul turned away and began walking down the dirt road in the direction of the lake, towards the main road where he would take a right turn, going back in the direction of Magdala and to the rental stables that he'd seen as they were entering the town.

The trip back to Jerusalem was uneventful. Saul made an effort to get back as quickly as possible. He wasn't accustomed to traveling by himself, particularly through the mountain passes and desert roads which he'd only seen for the first time when he left Jerusalem with Jeshua and the disciples approximately five weeks earlier. He rode on his horse in a southerly direction and spent quiet evenings meditating in the rooms that he rented at inns or boarding houses along the way.

Saul gave considerable thought to the words that Jeshua shared with him as they were saying farewell. He wondered what Jeshua meant, as to what the future held in store, but as Jeshua said, in time the future shall become the present, and he would learn soon enough.

Chapter 21
The Miracles

Saul wanted to continue receiving information regarding Jeshua, during the long periods in between their visits, so he occasionally made it a point of visiting the home of Lazarus and his two sisters, Martha and Mary. It was on a pleasant Sunday morning following the Sabbath that Saul decided to take a long walk from the market place, northerly to the road to Bethany. He passed the inn where he had met Jeshua several years earlier, when he was first introduced to the family from Magdala.

Saul enjoyed the walk on the way to their home, past the olive and fig tree groves, farms and fields and gentle rolling hills. At times dogs would come scurrying towards him, sticking their heads between fence posts as they stood on their side of the property,

barking ferociously, letting him know they were protecting their family and property. Saul was amused at their antics and sometimes would pretend to throw a rock at them, watching them run away from the fence, only to return barking with more intensity.

The walk along the road to Bethany was visually relaxing, for it was so different than the hubbub and chaos in Jerusalem, that the serenity and sparseness of the locations of the homes on the properties, added to the solitude and quietness that enfolded during his trip. In his mind, he compared it with his childhood where he had also grown up in the suburb of a city and realized the tremendous differences in the scenery. Outside of Tarsus, there were rolling green hills and the mountain ranges could be seen in the distance from the lush valley that he knew so well from his childhood adventures.

But here in Bethany, the land was flatter, and the hills to the south would not be considered mountains, and it didn't have the greenery and vegetation that he had been accustomed to. After walking very slowly for about thirty minutes after passing the inn, he found himself standing in front of the property of the Magdalene family. He didn't see anyone outside, so he entered through the gate walking towards the house which was set back about forty yards from the road.

As he got closer, he noticed that Lazarus was in the back yard feeding the hens and that he was throwing seeds on the ground in front of them that he was pulling from a sack that he carried in his left hand. Upon seeing Saul, he said, "Saul, welcome, welcome. We have not seen you for a while. How have you been?"

Saul walked up to Lazarus and since both of Lazarus' hands were occupied, Saul placed his left hand on the shoulder of this tall, lanky man, and gave it a slight squeeze in friendship. "I'm fine Lazarus. It's good to see you. Are your sister's home also?" "Yes they are. Martha, Mary, come and see who is here," shouted Lazarus.

Several seconds later, Martha and Mary both emerged from the back door of the house, only a few feet from where Lazarus and Saul were standing. Both of the women, upon seeing Saul, walked over to him very quickly and took turns hugging him. "Well stranger, it has been a few months since we've seen you. What have you been up to?" asked Martha.

"Nothing of great importance. It was such a beautiful day, I thought I would take a walk to Bethany to pay my respects to all of you and see if you have any news of Jeshua." "Girls, why don't you sit on the bench in front of the house, serve some spiced water or wine to our guest, and you can bring him up to date regarding the latest news on Jeshua. Martha, give him a slice of the delicious honey cake you baked last night. The boy looks starved," Lazarus said.

The three of them laughed and Martha turned to go back into the house while Mary took Saul by the arm and led him around to the front of the house. They both sat down at the wooden table opposite each other. A few moments later Martha came out the front door carrying a tray which held slices of honey cake and three cups. She also carried a pitcher of spiced wine.

"This is very gentle wine, for I mixed it with other fruit juices. You'll find it very refreshing Saul, and it won't blur your vision, so

you won't get lost on the way home," Martha jokingly said as she set the tray and pitcher on the table in front of them. Saul then asked, "So what is the news, ladies? Do you have any information regarding what's going on with Jeshua? It's been over a year since I visited with him on our trip to Capernaum."

Mary answered, "Yes, we do have some information. Some of the information comes from friends and neighbors who know him from Capernaum. Other information comes from some of the disciples who visited Jerusalem recently, as well as Thomas, the disciple who was originally from Cyrene and who now lives in Jerusalem. They've shared with us some incredible stories of some of the things that Jeshua is doing, which can only fall into the category of being miracles."

"Mary, tell Saul about the wine," Martha said. Mary, with her beautiful eyes and dimpled cheeks, looked into Saul's eyes and said, "Saul, I don't know how you're going to take this information because it doesn't sound real, but yet those who told us the stories, swear that they are true.

"They tell us that Jeshua was attending a wedding in Cana, where one of his cousins was getting married. There were over a hundred guests there and the activities and partying lasted two days, the day of the ceremony as well as the day after. We were told that early in the afternoon of the second day, they ran out of wine, and were frantically trying to find more, to avoid being embarrassed in front of the guests."

Martha then jumped in, saying, "And Saul, you can't believe what happened. In hearing about the problem, Jeshua instructed the waiters to pour water into the empty vats that had contained the wine. He then told them to pour the water from the vats into pitchers in order to serve the guests. But when they poured it into the pitchers, it was no longer water, but it was wine that was being poured. Wine that tasted as good as the best wine you could ever find in Galilee, and there was no end to it."

Mary excitedly added, "Whenever they needed more, Jeshua told them to pour more water into the vats, and then into the pitchers and more wine came out every time." Martha then said, "How can this be accounted for? It is a miracle! An absolute miracle! Jeshua had performed a miracle." Saul didn't answer, only nodded his head in acknowledgment of the story they had told. Saul was thinking that Jeshua indeed had performed a miracle. "But it doesn't end there Saul. Mary, tell him what else happened on the hillside overlooking Galilee."

Again Mary looked into the eyes of Saul and said, "A huge number of people had gathered on the hillside at the northern end of town overlooking the lake. There had to be more than five hundred people easily, we are told. Jeshua stood at the high point of the hillside, while the others sat on the ground facing him, with their backs towards the lake.

"Jeshua spoke to them for two hours, teaching them his messages and explaining their relationship with God. They then realized it was lunch time and none of them had brought any food with them, except that several people had loaves of bread, as well as several baskets of kipper, which are only this big," holding her fingers about four inches apart, "that they had gotten from the Sea of Galilee."

Mary continued with amazement in her voice, "Jeshua instructed some of the disciples who were there, to retrieve the baskets of bread and fishes and they wandered among the people, handing each person a couple of the fish and pieces of the bread. And even though there were more than five hundred people there, the baskets never became empty. Each time they reached in for more fish or bread, it seems that the food was replenishing itself."

Martha then added, "Saul, more than five hundred people were fed from those two baskets of bread and two baskets of fish, as if there were actually over a hundred baskets. We were told that the people sat in amazement and shock as Jeshua just stood there with a loving smile on his face, not saying a word." Mary then asked, "How do you explain this Saul? It is a miracle, for there is no other explanation."

Saul listened carefully and again did not say a word, but only nodded his head in acknowledgment that he understood what they were sharing with him. Finally, after about fifteen seconds of silence, Saul said, "Yes, there aren't any other explanations other than Jeshua is performing miracles."

Mary said, "Saul, there's more information also, but I don't know all the facts. You told us last time you were here that Thomas had given you directions to his home and had agreed to let you see him, if you chose. He can give you more information, and tell you about some of the other miracles that we've heard about."

"Yes, I will go see Thomas. I want to hear everything that I can about these miracles that Jeshua's performing." The three then sat for another half an hour, enjoying the honey cake and wine, and sharing gossip between themselves. Saul then thanked them for their hospitality, and the three of them walked to the back of the house so Saul could say goodbye to Lazarus.

On his walk back to Jerusalem, Saul was deep in thought about the things that had been shared with him. He wondered if there could be any other explanation for the stories he heard, or if they were exactly as Martha and Mary had described to him. Assuming the stories were true, he then wondered why Jeshua would now be performing these incredible acts, since he hadn't done so in the past. He would make it a point of seeing Thomas, so he could find out as much information about the miracles as he could.

Saul decided he wouldn't wait until the next day, but would visit Thomas that very afternoon. Shortly after the lunch hour, Saul made his way from his home in the upper city, down the hill to the marketplace. Upon arriving at the marketplace, he found the usual chaos and excitement of the many hundreds of people shopping and milling around the various stalls and watching the activities.

This would have been the third time he visited Thomas' home. He followed the directions that Thomas had given to him during their stroll along the Sea of Galilee, and soon found himself walking east of the marketplace through the streets of the smaller, densely populated areas. It was not long before he was standing in front of the house of Thomas and knocked on the door loudly, hoping to find Thomas at home.

After a few moments, he heard the rustling of feet coming towards the door and Thomas opened it. He immediately recognized Saul, and looked at him without any expression, and said over his

shoulder as he turned away, "Follow me." He shuffled his way into the room immediately to the right of the hallway, which was the kitchen. He motioned to Saul to sit on a chair at the kitchen table as he walked over to the stove where he had been heating water in a pot.

The pot was sitting on an iron plate that was sitting over an open utensil that was filled with oil that had been lit. Without saying another word, he poured the hot water into two cups which held a number of herbs that gave off a pleasant aroma as the hot water was poured onto them. He passed a cup to Saul as he sat down.

Saul then said, "Thomas, this morning I visited with Martha and Mary and they shared stories with me of some of the events that are happening in Jeshua's life in Galilee. I'm sure that you heard about the wedding in Cana, where Jeshua transformed water into wine. And then there's the story of the people that he fed on the hillside overlooking Galilee, even though he started with a small amount of bread and fish, and the people were supposedly in the hundreds. You have heard of these stories, have you not?"

"Yes Saul. I have heard these stories, and although I wasn't there, I believe that they are true. I have heard them from a number of people, some who were actually witnesses to both events. But there are even more stories that are more wonderful and miraculous than those" Saul responded, "Thomas, I want to know everything that you can tell me. Share with me the other stories that you've heard or seen for yourself."

Thomas had both his hands around the cup that was sitting before him, and he stared as if he was studying the contents with great interest. He was trying to form his thoughts, so he could present them to Saul in the most credible manner that he could. "I'll tell you the stories exactly as I heard them or as I saw them myself."

Thomas put both his elbows on the table and still holding his cup with both hands, held it just below his chin. Saul noticed that he was staring straight ahead, with his eyes not focused, as if he was trying to visualize the events in his mind that he had either seen or heard.

He then continued, "Everything I am sharing with you has happened within the last six months. Jeshua was leaving the temple in Capernaum, where he had been speaking and the temple was packed, for he had been drawing huge crowds. As he was leaving, there was a man sitting on his knees to the right of the pathway that lead away from the steps of the temple, who appeared to be a crippled beggar. As Jeshua approached him, he pleaded with Jeshua to help him, and asked God for mercy."

Thomas hesitated, as if he was again visualizing the scene in his mind, then continued, "Jeshua stopped and put his right hand on the man's forehead and said something to the effect of, 'You are forgiven for your sins. God loves you and I love you, and you are now healed.' The man looked up at Jeshua with amazement and slowly pushed himself up onto his feet and began walking in a circle. Then he began to shout and yell with joy that he had been healed. That Jeshua had healed him."

Saul didn't ask any questions, for he just wanted to listen to the stories of these miracles. He said, "Go on." Thomas continued, "Word spread through the crowd like wild fire and people had begun to shout that Jeshua had healed the crippled beggar. Then a

man came up to him and said, 'Jeshua, I have a child at home who I fear is dying. She is very sick, and her mother and I are beyond ourselves, for we don't know what to do. Can you please come and pray for her?'

Jeshua looked at the man and put his hands on his shoulders and asked if he believed that his child could be healed with God's will. The man answered that he did and then Jeshua said, 'Take me to your daughter.' Jeshua then followed the man as they walked a short distance to the man's house. When they arrived, they went into the house where the little girl was laying, surrounded by her mother and several other women who were crying. Peter was also with him. Jeshua went over to the child and knelt down on his knees beside the bed, kissed her on the forehead and said something to the effect that God loved her and she was now healed."

Thomas was still staring ahead of him with his eyes not focused, but seeming as if they were looking into another dimension, and Saul noticed that tears had filled his eyes. He continued, "The child opened her eyes and smiled and sat up in bed. All the women started crying and wailing with joy. I was told that the man then ran into another room and came back with a pouch of coins and tried to give them to Jeshua, but Jeshua said to him, 'God does not need your money. Only your love and faith,' and then he turned and walked outside the room and back into the street." Saul sat in total silence, as he took in all of Thomas' words. After a few seconds he said, "Tell me everything that you know Thomas, please."

"That was just the beginning Saul. As word got around, more and more people who were sick either came or were carried to Jeshua, and Jeshua healed them one after another. He healed people who were blind, people who were deaf, people who were crippled, and people who were sick and appeared to be dying. He then began to travel to some of the other villages and towns in Galilee and performed healings in each of those places.

"I can't tell you the total number of people who were healed, only that there was one miracle after another, after another. I personally witnessed some of them, and others were told to me by others who were witnesses. They are all true Saul. These are not like some of the stories in the Holy Book where you don't know if they are real or not. These stories are true."

Saul searched for words to say, but was so overwhelmed from the stories and the thoughts going through his mind, that before he could respond, Thomas then said, "There is something else too Saul. You know that John ben Zacharia, the one they call John the Baptist who we saw that day when we traveled to the Jordan River with Jeshua, he is now dead?"

Thomas continued, "The king, Herod Antapis persuaded the wife of his brother Phillip, Herodius, to divorce Phillip so that she could marry Herod. You know what he did is against the Judaic law and people have been furious, but they wouldn't say so publicly. But John, he continued to publicly condemn Herod and Herodius for this disgusting act, and he was warned time and again to stop doing so. But one day along the river while he was preaching, there were the special guardsmen of Herod there and John made it a point of attacking Herod again, and he was arrested. Not too long after, he was put to death." Saul said sadly, "Yes, I know about the death of

John ben Zacharia."

Thomas responded, "Well, Jeshua met with some of his disciples in Caesarea Philippi in Upper Galillee a few months ago after the death of John, and after he had been doing healings. I was told this story by both John and Matthew, who were both there. Jeshua asked the disciples who people were saying that he was, and they answered him that some were saying that he was the prophet Elijah which had been prophesized five hundred years earlier in the Holy Book in the chapter written by Malachi, that the prophet Elijah would be born again.

The Holy Book stated that Elijah would be born again with the coming of the Messiah. Jeshua answered to them that he was not Elijah and that he who had been Elijah in a past life had already come and that they didn't recognize him, and that he had been killed, just as surely as he would also someday suffer the same. They all knew that he was speaking of John ben Zacharia, that Jeshua was saying that John was the one who had been Elijah. And that Elijah had to come before he came."

Thomas's eyes now focused on Saul, with an expression on his face as if he were expecting a response. Saul then said, "Yes, it makes sense. I remember at the River Jordan, as Jeshua was approaching John in the water, John yelled out to the people, 'I am here to show you the way. And this man is the way.' Yes, I understand now. The prophet Elijah was born again as John to introduce the Messiah, just as it is stated in our Holy Book, in the last chapter, in Malachi."

Saul let out a big sigh, as if the stories were so astonishing and incredible, that he couldn't absorb all the information. "Is there anything else that you can tell me at this time? Or have you covered everything?" Thomas answered, "One other thing. I recall hearing that some of the religious authorities had also gone to John the Baptist and had asked him if he had been the prophet Elijah in a previous lifetime, and I am told that John gave them a confusing answer, which they didn't understand." Thomas took a few moments to give some more thought, and then said "I can't think of anything else Saul."

Many years later, when some of the disciples would write testimonials as to what took place during the life of Jeshua, Matthew described the incident regarding Jeshua meeting with the disciples in the 16th Chapter of his gospel, beginning on line 13 and in Chapter 17, line 9, just as Thomas had described to Saul. Also, in John's testimonial, on Chapter 1, lines 19 through 24, he described in his testament the incident of the officials asking John the Baptist if he was the reincarnation of the prophet Elijah.

Both Saul and Thomas stood up and Saul reached across the table, placing his left hand on Thomas' shoulder, "Thank you, Thomas. Thank you for sharing the information with me." Saul turned to his left and walked out of the kitchen into the entryway and then took another left and went out the front door. As he walked from the house back in the direction of the marketplace, as well as through the marketplace, he was totally oblivious to the hundreds of people who were milling around him and all the activities.

He couldn't hear the shouts of the sellers from their stalls, the collective chattering of people bargaining with the sellers, or the

shrill voices of the children playing in the background. He walked through the crowd at the marketplace as if he were in a vacuum and his mind and his thoughts were solely channeled on what had been shared with him from Martha and Mary and now confirmed by Thomas, as he tried to process and understand what he had heard.

He continued in this mode as he walked through the marketplace in the lower city and began the slow climb up the hill to his home in the upper city. He purposely took a path in which there were very few houses and was very quiet, so that he wouldn't be disturbed in his contemplation.

When he finally reached his home, he sat outside on the stone bench overlooking the lower city, still in awe, trying to comprehend and process the information. Later that night as he lay in his bed, with his last thoughts before he fell into a deep slumber, he prayed that Jeshua would soon be in Jerusalem, so they could be together.

Chapter 22
The Discussion

Two months had not yet passed, when a messenger came to the house of Saul, notifying him that Jeshua had returned to Jerusalem. The messenger told him that Jeshua would meet him at noon time north of the garden of Gethsemani, outside the walls of the city, at the intersection of the two roads that connect the Golden Gate entrance and the Sheep Gate entrance into the city. As usual, in his excitement of being with Jeshua, Saul arrived before him. Jeshua arrived shortly after and this time he was alone.

As Jeshua approached Saul, he noticed that Jeshua looked thinner and not as well rested as he had been in the past. It immediately occurred to Saul that recently Jeshua had been under tremendous pressure, with the healings and the tremendous numbers of people

that Saul had heard were following him everywhere he went. When Jeshua reached him, the two men immediately embraced, without saying a word to one another.

As they parted, Jeshua smiled at Saul and said "How are you my dear friend? It's good to see you again." "And you too Jeshua", responded Saul. "Come Saul, let's head north, into the Kidron Valley. We'll take a hike and find some pleasant place for us to sit and talk."

The two men left the roadway, and began to walk on a foot path that led them onto the eastern side of the valley. The path became steeper and steeper as they climbed higher up the mountainside. Saul, walking behind Jeshua, noticed the strength in his wiry but muscular calves as Jeshua climbed in front of Saul, the two of them sometimes having to pull themselves up higher by grabbing a hold of brush along side of the trail.

When they finally reached about two thirds of the way up the mountain side, Jeshua motioned toward a large flat rock and said "Why don't we sit here, and rest and enjoy the view." The two men sat down on the flat rock, with Jeshua on Saul's right, and took in the view of the valley directly before them, in a westerly direction. The land was steep, not only on the side where they were sitting, but also on the other side of the valley, which was fairly close to them, so they could easily see the vegetation directly across from them. Directly below them was a river which was fast running and very narrow, due to the steepness of the slopes on either side.

After they had caught their breath, Jeshua said "What have you been up to Saul? Bring me up to date." Saul answered "It certainly has been awhile since we last saw each other Jeshua. And it was almost eight years ago that you took me to the Jordan River that day, where I saw your cousin John ben Zachariah speaking to the people along the shore. I feel so terrible about his death Jeshua. I am so sorry for you and your family."

Saul turned to Jeshua, and noticed that his eyes had moistened. "Yes, it was a great sadness to us all. It was so unnecessary. John not being here is a tremendous loss to everybody. It has been several years Saul, since you joined me on one of my trips from Jerusalem to Capernaum. I'm told that you've visited with Mary and her sister and brother several times since then, as well as with my disciple, Thomas. I'm pleased that you have kept in touch with them. How old are you now Saul? I know that you were twenty when we first met, but I've lost track of how many years ago that has been."

Saul said, "It was ten years ago Jeshua. I'm thirty now, and I assume you are still two years older than I am, or have you aged faster or slower than I have?" Both men laughed at Saul's attempt at humor and then Saul continued "Jeshua, I've heard stories of what you've been doing. I'm told that you've been healing people that are sick, and doing many other things that others have described as miracles. There's tremendous excitement in Jerusalem, people wanting to be healed, and many others that want to see you doing the healing. You weren't doing healings when I last saw you. What has changed since then?"

Jeshua picked up a small rock and dropped it in front of him and the two of them watched it roll down the mountain. He then turned to Saul and said "I was very disappointed that many people were not

accepting what I was sharing with them. I would try to explain to them their relationship with God, and many times they would not embrace the words I was sharing with them. They didn't know me and didn't know if I was worthy to justify that the messages that I shared with them were worth their accepting. I decided to do the healings Saul, so I could have more and more people understand my relationship with God, and more important, their relationship with God."

Saul responded by saying "And I know that has worked Jeshua. Everybody in Jerusalem now knows who you are. There are some that say you are using sorcery, and are not to be taken seriously, for they're jealous of your powers, or just don't believe it could be true. Then there are others that are saying you're a prophet, or that you are the anointed one, the messiah that was predicted would come to show the way. Otherwise, they ask, how could you have these powers?"

Jeshua thought for a moment and then responded," I have no power that isn't available to all the children of God. You have heard me say a number of times that the goal of our journey is to become at one with that part inside of us that is God. Saul, when people achieve that, when people become at one with God, then all of God's children will have the same powers that are attributed to me. They'll be able to heal themselves rather then relying on me to be a conduit for them. They'll know that they have the spirit of God within them, and have the same power. The same force which has the ability to create life also has the ability to sustain health.

"They'll recognize that much of their sickness was a cause from within, from their own sins and self infliction. And they will learn that they have the ability to forgive themselves for their sins, for it's they that have caused their own illness. They will understand that they have the power through the spirit of God that resides within them to cure their illness and be well.

"As for me, I am helping them heal themselves, but this can only happen if they believe that they are capable of being healed, and they acknowledge and understand that the spirit of God does reside within them. If they don't believe that Saul, they can't heal themselves and I can't help them."

Saul responds, "Jeshua, please be very careful. I'm concerned about your welfare. If you do healings in Galilee, there is no one going to bother you there. But here in Jerusalem, there are the religious leaders who are very jealous of the stories that they've heard of your healings and your miracles. And also, the Roman authorities I am told, are concerned about the tremendous number of people who are your followers. I am told that they are concerned that if you do the same things in Jerusalem, as you've done in Galilee and Samaria, that you will have huge followings of people, and that they will not have control over you or them. Please don't alienate them."

"I understand Saul", Jeshua said," but it's all right. You must understand. You cannot destroy an idea of God." Saul looked very distraught. He turned to Jeshua and with a great deal of concern and sadness in his voice he asked, "But Jeshua, you must be concerned over alienating the Romans, as well as the religious authorities. Do you think that is wise?"

Jeshua looked into the eyes and soul of Saul, and answered "You ask if that is wise. You ask if I have concern of alienating others, as I speak the words of God. No, I don't have concerns.. If I speak the words of God Saul, I can't have fear or concerns over those who choose not to accept what is truth."

Saul processed these profound words that Jeshua said to him, and the two of them sat for many minutes in silence, both deep in thought. Finally, Jeshua stood up and turned to Saul and smiled with that beautiful smile that wiped away Saul's sadness and concerns, and he said "Come Saul, it's time for us to return. I must do the work of our father."

They were silent as they worked their way back down the mountain along the path that they had climbed. When they finally reached the bottom of flat ground, they returned to the intersection of the roads to the gates where they had met. Jeshua then turned to Saul and said "Tomorrow mid-morning I'll be speaking at the temple. My pupils have been going through the city inviting people to join me. Then later I'll be at the central well at the marketplace, where I will do healings here in Jerusalem. I hope you'll be there, both at the Temple as well as at the well."

Saul smiled and said "Yes Jeshua, I will be there." The two men embraced, and went their separate directions, Jeshua going westward, to connect to the road to Bethany, and Saul going eastward, to the road leading through the Golden Gate, to begin his journey across the temple grounds and into the upper city.

As Saul left the temple grounds, and found himself on the western edge of the upper city, he realized he would be passing a short distance from the home of Rabbi Gamaill, and he decided he would stop and visit with him. He made it a point of seeing his old teacher several times a year, and it had been several months since they had last talked. He decided that it would be helpful if he could have Rabbi Gamaill give him his opinion regarding if Jeshua's actions had placed him in a dangerous position with the Roman authorities or the religious leaders.

When Saul got to the gate of the rabbi's property, he passed through and approached the house, since Gamaill was not outside. He noticed the house, like Gamaill's health, looked as though it was in need of repair, and was not in the best condition. Saul walked up to the door and knocked very loudly, calling out Gamaill's name.

After a few moments the door opened and a big smile appeared on Saul's face which happened almost automatically, every time he saw the rabbi. He looked down at his dear friend who was short in stature, and who resembled an owl, with his round face and big round brown eyes, and his short scrubby beard and his portly belly.

"Saul, how are you my boy. How is my favorite pupil doing? Come, come let's go sit on the bench outside under the tree, where we can talk. Can I bring you anything to eat or drink?"

Saul turned and began walking towards the bench with Gamaill keeping pace on his immediate left. "No, rabbi, I don't need food or drink. What I really need is your insight and wisdom." The two men sat opposite each other and looked into each other's eyes "Saul, what's troubling you? You look like you have the weight of the world on your shoulders?"

"It's prophesied in the Holy Books that someday the messiah

would come, and would lead the Israelites. Are we to take the words of a prophet hundreds of years ago seriously?" Saul asked. Gamaill answered, "When you talk of the words that are in the Holy Writings, it requires good judgment to determine what is truth and what is fable. Did you know Saul, it's written in the First Book of Chronicles, in Chapter 21, that King David took a census in order to determine how many men were capable of fighting in the war?

"And it states then that God was so angry at David taking the census that the lord proceeded to have seventy thousand Israeli men die by pestilence, as punishment against David. Now Saul, do you really think that God would kill seventy thousand innocent men because he is mad at David for taking a census, or do you think perhaps the chronicler, the man who wrote Chronicles, that he was the one that was upset, for perhaps either his name or the name of one of his sons might have been included in the census?"

Saul then asked, "I understand what you're saying rabbi. But getting back to the prophets, how were they in the position to know what is going to happen in the future? How are they able to make these prophecies?" Gamaill answered, "There are some people who have this gift, and that is why they are called prophets. It is as if they are standing on a tall hill, and you are standing directly below them. They can look behind you and see where you have been. Then they can look down upon you and see where are now, and they can look in front of you and see the path that you are going to take. And it's through this gift of being able to see the past, present and the future that allows them to give their prophecies."

Saul then asked, "But are they always right? I don't think they are always right, do you think so rabbi?" Gamaill responded, "Often times Saul, a person will proceed with their life in which there are very little decisions to be made, until they come to a crossroad. Through the gift of free will that God has given to them, they may choose a different path at that crossroad, then the prophets thought they would choose.

"You yourself Saul, you have had several crossroads in your life. There were very little decisions for you to make until you chose as a young man, to leave Tarsus and come to the Holy Land. Had you chose not to leave Tarsus, your life would be entirely different, would it not? And you told me of your love for Leah. Had you made the decision to marry her, perhaps rather than sitting here talking to me now, you would be home bouncing two children on your lap. So no Saul, the future is not carved in stone, because others who are in your life may influence you, or you yourself may make a decision that causes you to choose a different path, then you otherwise might have."

Saul then looked into the eyes of Gamaill with great concern and said "I'm sure you heard of the miracles that Jeshua is doing. I was with him earlier today, and he'll be speaking at the temple grounds tomorrow, and then begin doing healings here in Jerusalem, for the first time, tomorrow afternoon. I know that there will be huge crowds that will be there, for the word has spread throughout Judea of his healings. Please share with me rabbi, is the feeling of great concern that I have within my heart justified in that he may be placing himself in danger?"

Gamaill closed his eyes in deep thought and was silent for a very

long period of time. He finally opened his eyes and responded "Saul, you must understand that the Romans are absolute in demanding and requiring control of the people. If they consider any person being a threat to them perhaps because they have a tremendous following of people, and the Romans feel that they don't have control over that individual who is their leader, than indeed that person would be in danger.

"That is why they look toward the Sanhedrin to have control over the people in Jerusalem, as well as other parts of Israel that they occupy. They rely on the Sanhedrin to control the people and in turn the Sanhedrin are responsible to the Romans to see that there are no uprisings or rebellions, and that the people pay their annual taxes to the Romans in an orderly manner. The Romans make no exception to demanding that they have those controls."

Saul then asked, "What is the worst that can happen to a person such as Jeshua, who may have thousands of people as his followers, and as you describe, he doesn't answer to religious authorities or to anybody else, except to God?" Gamaill answered very solemnly "You already know that answer Saul. How many of our people do the Romans kill every year, in order to show their strength and to maintain their control? They don't care about taking a life of a Jew if it serves their purpose. If they feel threatened at all, they will act against Jeshua."

Saul asked "You mean kill him, don't you?" Again, Gamaill answered Saul "When the Romans feel that someone is a threat to their authority, they will not only kill him, but they will use his death as an example to others. Is there anything crueler than crucifixion?

What greater way to set an example by the Romans then to have a public crucifixion of anybody that they feel is undermining their authority and their power?"

Saul, sat quietly for a few moments feeling the dread enter into his body and touch every nerve. He then asked, "Is Jeshua a threat to the Sanhedrin also? Could they have him punished if they feel he's a threat to them also?" Gamaill responded, "The Sanhedrin are responsible for the civil laws of Judea that can bring a person to trial for stealing, trespassing, not paying their debts. I would imagine they would find it difficult to accuse Jeshua of having committed a civil crime.

"Yes, he has healed people on the Sabbath, and therefore has violated our Sabbath day, but who is going to bring charges against him, the people that he is healing? The members of the Sanhedrin would find it very difficult to oppose the people, to try to punish Jeshua because he is healing people on the Sabbath. They don't like what he is saying regarding some of the activities that are taking place within the temple.

"Yes Saul, I have heard how over a year ago he entered the temple grounds and turned over the tables of the money changers, as well as knocked over the cages that held animals that were to be sacrificed within the temple. But there are many people who agree with him, that they should not allow exchanging the Roman coins for Jewish coins so the money can be brought into the temple to pay the priests.

There are many people who agree that the money changers should not be working on the temple grounds, and to sacrifice animal

at the alter in the temple has nothing to do with God's will. No Saul, although the Sanhedrin and other religious authorities may dislike passionately the remarks that Jeshua makes when he is criticizing them, I don't see them bringing action against Jeshua. Only the Romans could hurt Jeshua physically and that is where your concerns should be."

The two men continued to discuss the likelihood of Jeshua reaching the point of being such a threat to the Romans that they would take action against him. But, they also both agreed that they couldn't look toward the Sanhedrin to have any influence on the Romans, should the Romans decide to take action against Jeshua. There would be no reason for the religious authorities to try to protect Jeshua against the Romans. Nor would Jeshua be willing to choose to restrain himself by not doing his miracles publicly, and only by Jeshua restraining himself and not doing his miracles publicly, could he avoid the possible consequences from the Romans.

But they both agreed this is probably unlikely that it would deter Jeshua. The two men finally said goodbye as the sun was slowly disappearing in the west and the sky began to darken, both sharing great concern in their eyes, and Gamaill feeling compassion in his heart for Saul's sadness. Saul then continued in deep thought as he traveled the rest of the distance in the upper city to his home.

His final thoughts as he lay in bed, were of great anticipation and the excitement of being able to hear the words of Jeshua at the temple the next day and then to see the healings. But this excitement was also intermingled with anxieties and fear for Jeshua's safety because of these same acts. Yes, tomorrow would be quite a day.

Chapter 23
The Temple Sermon

Saul entered the grounds of the temple, through its southern gate, into the court of the Gentiles. The sun had not reached full height, and since it was in the colder months of the year, he knew that Jeshua would be speaking in front of the crowd on the southern side of the temple, where the people would be warmer.

As he approached the stairs he saw that many hundreds of people were gathered, some sitting on the marble stairs and some standing and milling around at the marble landing below the first step. There were people of all kinds of descriptions and unlike the early times when Jeshua began speaking, it appeared to Saul that approximately twenty-five to thirty percent of the people that were gathered were women.

Saul thought to himself that the people that are gathered are truly a cross section of Jerusalem. There were elderly men in long white

beards, and there were others that were dressed as fairly well to do professional people, both men and women. On the outskirts, those standing appeared to be some that had the bearing and attire of being members of the religious authorities as well their scribes. There were also poorer people. There were some that were shoeless, wearing course ill fitting tunics, stained and needing mending, contrary to those of the wealthier class that were dressed in a festive mood, as if they were attending a social function.

Saul noticed that there were no children, but the women collectively appeared to be younger than most of the men, appearing to be in their teenage years or in their twenties. However, even though the courtyard behind him was referred to as the Court of the Gentiles, where the pagans were allowed to sell their birds and other small animals for sacrifice, he noticed only very few individuals among the huge crowd appeared not to be Jews. It made sense to Saul that very few Gentiles would have an interest in hearing what Jeshua had to say, even those who also believed in pagan gods.

Saul recognized only a handful of people that he knew, and after about a half an hour the crowd that had gathered, at Saul's estimate, there were hundreds of people. It was at that time that Jeshua appeared, even though no one had recognized his entrance into the courtyard and his approach to the stairs. Unlike every other time when Jeshua was to address his audience standing below them, or from the marble slab in front of the stairs, the people sat on the stairway and instead Jeshua climbed the stairs so he was now standing very close to the top of the stairway, where he could look down upon all the people. The crowd gathered around him in a fan shape with Jeshua standing at the apex.

Saul seated himself to Jeshua's right, approximately six steps lower than from where Jeshua was standing. The crowd was so enormous, that it was impossible for Saul to make eye contact with Jeshua. There was tremendous excitement among the crowd that it sounded as if hundreds of people were talking simultaneously, as they began to arrange themselves so they in turn would be facing Jeshua as they stood to the side and below him.

Jeshua looked magnificent, standing with great serenity, looking down upon the people, with the sun creating golden highlights in his hair. He was wearing an off color white robe made of very soft material, that stopped just above his ankles, in which the sleeves were open and stopped just above his wrist. His eyes were clear, and his face radiated both strength and beauty, as he silently looked over his audience.

Several minutes went by, in which the sound got quieter and quieter, until there was total silence. And now Jeshua began to speak in a melodious voice that was resonant and yet filled with so much passion, that every person felt that he was talking personally to them.

He said, "Everything that is important to you in life, including your need to be loved and accepted, is all contained within you. Everything that you need, in trying to understand your relationship with God, lies within. For within you is a store room that contains many wonderful things. Each one of you has a key that will open the door to that store room. You may enter into it and take what is yours and visit it as often as you choose to, once you understand that it is a gift that you have all received in being part of God that is inside of

each and every one of you."

Jeshua waited a few seconds so that what he was saying could be processed by the people. He looked around his audience and then continued, "There is a wisdom and spiritual mind internally that most times you refrain from trying to communicate with. Yes, it is difficult to center with your spiritual mind so you can be in tune with it. But if you are not aware of it, or at best, if you are not making an effort to be in touch with it, it is impossible to become at one with it. Being at one with it brings happiness and understanding, for it will become obvious to you that there are so many things that you worry about in life that are not material, for they have nothing to do with happiness.

"So you must look within, for the greatest gifts you have are internal. You must learn to center yourselves. You must learn to find your soul mind. It is there for each and every one of you to share and find peace. If you open a channel you shall see and shall understand, for it is within every one of you who are God's children."

As Jeshua now stood in silence looking at the throngs of people before him, there was a slight murmuring as people were making remarks among themselves, then finally a voice yelled out "You say these things are inside of us Jeshua. How do we find them?" Jeshua looked in the direction of the person who spoke and said, "I say to you that indeed, there is a treasure chest inside of every one of you and you do have the ability to find the key and open the chest and enjoy the wonderful things within the treasure chest, for they are yours."

An elderly man then yelled out, in a voice what was wobbly and almost shrill, "How do you describe God, rabbi? How can we visualize our being part of God? I don't understand." Jeshua eyes sought out the individual who called out this question who was seated about 12 rows below him, slightly to his left, and having found him, he answered, "Even though we refer to God as the father, God is both our father and our mother, for God has no single gender.

God is a force, an entity of love and life that all of us are a part of. Think of a body of water, like a lake. That lake, for purposes of understanding, think of it as an energy force of love and wisdom and knowledge. Each drop of that lake is part of the whole. If we take a jar and dip it into the lake, which is made up of thousands and thousands of little drops of water, they are part of the whole of the lake.

"We then scatter the drops in different places. Each little drop is put into the body of a newborn. These infants would then be a part of that lake, even if they do not recognize it. That little portion of the lake that is within them enables them to be eternal and everlasting. It is what gives you life. Now if we equate that lake instead to being God, a different form of energy rather than the lake, then you have a better understanding that you are part of God, just as the drop of water was part of the lake. If that drop of water was to return eventually to that lake, it would then be again at one with the rest of the lake. So it is when spirit becomes at one again with the whole, someday, not only in thought, but physically, that we are again with God."

Saul turned his head, and looked down at the faces of the people that were sitting below him, and saw that they were enraptured. The

words of Jeshua were making a tremendous impact on them, and Saul could see that Jeshua's messages were literally touching their souls. Another voice, one that was strong and young boomed out at Jeshua. "Rabbi, I have heard you say before that we have the gift of free will. How does that affect our ability to become at one with God?"

Again, Jeshua looked in the direction of the person asking the question. He purposely waited a few moments and then answered in a voice filled with passion, strength and love, "God created you in his own image. He also gave you the will to choose your path on your way to reaching your destiny. The path that many of you have chosen unfortunately leads you further and further away from God, as well as from the truth. And now there are many of you who are lost.

"So many of you have been lead astray by desires of the senses, as well as your desires for gains in the material world. You must realize the material world itself can only give you gifts that are temporary, and has nothing of any lasting value. The kingdom of heaven lies within you, and God is within you also, residing within your own heart. God is everywhere and all of you are a part of one great spiritual family, for every one of you is a child of God. You must understand that and try to develop a feeling of unity with Oneness, knowing that indeed we are all one, and are manifestations of our omnipresent God."

Jeshua then broke into a beautiful smile and his eyes shone with a brightness as he continued, "Live in peace, live in love and be aware of the presence of God at all times. God is here, within you and outside of you and everywhere, and you yourself have a part of the spirit of God residing within you which gives you your divinity. You are the divine child of the omnipresent God."

A woman's voice could then be heard coming from one of the rows of stairs almost at the bottom near the marble slab. She asked, "Jeshua, what is the most important emotion or feeling we can have, is it peace or friendship?" Jeshua took one step further down as if he was trying to come into closer contact with the woman who had asked this question. And then he answered "Love is the motivating force for the universe, for love is God. Let love flow from you and see its illumination of power. The power of God through love transcends everything and can bring peace and tranquility to the troubled world.

"The laws of God are so simple. I say to each and every one of you, my brothers and sisters, it is so easy to understand what God is asking of you. And you do not need the permission of any other individual in order to obey the laws of God, and nor do you have to pay another individual in order to live this truth, whether it be a priest or in the temple. What God is asking of each and every one of you, is that you embrace universal love and universal compassion and live your lives in truth. If you are willing to do that, then surely you will realize that you are at one with God and will touch the lives of so many people, that they will also enjoy life though you."

A man yelled out "How about the priests Jeshua? They tell us that God's will is found through them, through their teachings and their efforts, through the sacrifices and the tithings that we pay to them, and the rituals that they teach us. They say that God is found here, in

this temple. How do you respond?"

A silence fell across the crowd, for they knew that based on Jeshua's answer he could be challenging the power and the influence of the religious authorities and the temple. Jeshua, in a very soft and yet almost angry voice answered, "You are the temple of God. If God resides within you, is it not true that you may hold your services with God it any time you choose, whether it be as you walk through a field, as you lie upon your own bed in the morning or before sleep, as you are shopping in the marketplace, and yes, as you take your temple into this temple that stands behind me? But God does not care about rituals. God does not care if you stand up or sit down while you are praying to him, nor does he ask you to memorize lines of words, which come from your mind, rather then your heart."

The crowd and Jeshua heard a voice cry out, a stern voice, as if it belonged to one of the priests, "Be careful Jeshua, be careful that you do not blasphemy. Have you come to judge us?"

Jeshua answered "I stand as an individual in the presence of God. I have come, not to judge you, but to help you." A few moments went by, and then Jeshua continued "I have come not to judge the world, but to save the world." Having said that, again commotion broke out that sounded like the voices of hundreds of people talking at once, responding to what Jeshua had just said.

A voice filled with hope and respect then called out "Jeshua, I have heard of the healings that you have done in Galilee and Samaria. Will you also be doing healings here in Jerusalem?"

Jeshua answered "Yes, God's love for you will also be manifested here in Jerusalem. I do the healings, as a conduit of God, to show the power of God that is contained within you and the love that God has for you, his children. I will be at the marketplace in the lower City, at the main well. Tell those who seek to be healed and who have faith and belief in the power of God, to come and join me in about two hours after noon. I leave you now, and may you continue to stand in God's light."

Having said that, Jeshua began to walk down the stairs. The crowd parted for him creating a pathway. As he walked past the people, many reached out and touched his arm, or a part of his clothing. Saul was now standing, and could see the faces of the people. Most were enraptured having been tremendously moved by the words that Jeshua shared with them. Some of the people in the outskirts of the crowd were talking amongst themselves, and appeared to be upset.

But the majority of the people had been thrilled, and began to follow Jeshua as the path closed behind him as he continued heading across to the Court of the Gentiles and through the exit adjacent to the Royal Portico. Saul stood on the stairway and watched the scene below with great pride. His heart beat with excitement, and finally when Jeshua was no longer in sight, he began to work his way through the people, down the stairway and into the courtyard.

He then eventually found his way down to the lower city. He was deep in thought and preferred to not have any company, but rather process the events that he had just witnessed, and to try to envision what would take place later that afternoon at the well in the marketplace. Yes, he thought to himself, this afternoon would be an extraordinary experience for all to witness.

Chapter 24
The Healings

Saul strolled around the bazaar an hour past noon time, knowing he had plenty of time to enjoy a leisurely meal before going to the well where Jeshua would perform the healings. He found a table in the rear of a quiet eating area, away from the crowd walking in both directions in between the rows of lined up shops and restaurants. Occasionally someone would walk by that recognized him and he would nod his head and smile at them, avoiding conversation.

He ordered a very light meal for he was not hungry. His mind was totally immersed into what he had witnessed earlier in the day at the temple, and what he imagined would take place at the well. He painfully thought of the possibility, what if nobody was healed? How would that affect Jeshua's credibility, and was that possible? Many thoughts raced through his mind until he finally realized that it

hy for him to be thinking that way. He cleared his mind
.ɛgative thoughts and instead imagined one healing after
another. People rejoicing and celebrating.

Saul finally pushed the half finished plate of food away from him
and began to slowly walk in the direction of the well. As he
approached the site, he saw that a huge crowd had gathered on all
four sides of the well. Several of the disciples were there and they
were separating the people, directing those who had come to be
healed on one side of the well, and the others either behind them or
to the opposite side of the well. Then they moved those that had
come for a healing back about ten feet from the well, leaving room
for Jeshua to walk in front of them in the space between them and
the well.

The crowd was excited and the air was filled with incredible
energy. Saul took a position behind those that were gathered to have
a healing so he could hear Jeshua's words better as well as see his
facial expressions while he did the healings. After about five minutes
went by, the crowd on the other side of the well parted, and Jeshua
appeared. He walked slowly around the perimeter of the well, until
he stood before the center of the crowd waiting for a healing.

There was total silence as Jeshua looked at those that stood before
him. He looked magnificent and radiant, his eyes sparking with love
and confidence. For a moment he made eye contact with Saul and a
very slight smile appeared on his face, as he continued to survey
those in front of him, the sick and the disabled and others with mild
ailments. And then he spoke.

"Dearest Lord. We all have received your miracle and wonder

called life. From your spirit we come forth to fulfill our relationship in the family of God. We all belong to your household dear God and we know you love each and every one of us as if we were your only child. Dear lord, open our hearts so we may hear you. May our hearts and souls recognize your voice and may the power of your Holy Spirit fall upon all of us, each one of us. And let us have faith in knowing that you are a loving God with the power to heal our minds, our bodies and our souls.

"Dear God, my beloved God, who is the creator of all that exists, open the hearts and souls of those before you, that they may receive your blessings. Now I ask those of you before me, do you not truly know that the spirit of God resides within you? You know with all your heart and soul that you are a child of God. You know that the greatest gift you have been given is that the spirit of God resides within you. It is the spirit of God that grants you everlasting life and immortality. For truly, since you are the child of our creator, in reality you are also a part of God. Just as God has the power to create, God also has the power to heal you."

Jeshua had now raised his voice. It was filled with great emotion and love. His head was tilted upwards as his eyes looked towards the heavens and he continually pleaded to God to heal those before him. Saul witnessed the jubilation, the joy and the bedlam that was taking place in front of him. As Jeshua continued in his asking God to heal his children, people were shouting out their healings, celebrating, crying and laughing all at the same time. A man who was partially crippled was leaping into the air and hopping on both legs; another man that had been almost totally blind was shouting, "I can see. I

can see."

A woman that was holding a young child in her arms was shouting, "He can hear. My child can hear." An elderly man that had been carried in the arms of his son was now walking on his two feet. And across the other side of the well, since it was only about knee high, those who were the family members and the friends of the people being healing were cheering and shouting out praises to God and Jeshua as they witnessed their loved ones being healed.

Paul watched these events unfold before him. Jeshua continued his asking God for healings, his arms stretched upwards towards the heavens, while his voice was drowned out by the shouts of joy by those being healed and the cheering from the crowd behind him. Saul lost all track of time. Now people had surrounded Jeshua, pressing against him, trying to touch him, to talk to him.

And he just stood there, majestically, with a loving gentle smile on his face, not moving, not responding, totally silent, totally still. Finally some of his disciples made their way to him, and separated the crowd from him. They created a pathway and led him away from the well, and flanked him on all sides as they lead him away from the crowd, into the streets of the lower city, possibly Saul thought, to the house where Thomas lived.

As Saul turned to leave, he noticed his friend, Talah, not far from him. He called out his name and when they made eye contact, he motioned to him. Talah, as always, was flamboyantly wearing his usual accessories of bracelets, necklaces and earrings on either side of his beardless face. As he approached Saul, the realization crossed Saul's mind as to why his handsome, almost feminine face, helped him in his favorite pastime, being popular with the young women in Jerusalem.

As he came within hearing distance of Saul, Talah said. "Did you see what I saw? How was that possible? It was incredible." "Let's go to some quiet area where we can talk. Let's go to that Moroccan cafe over there and have some spiced wine and talk," Saul responded as he pointed to his left. They pushed their way through the crowd that was still milling around and reached the outdoor area of the café after a couple of minutes.

They found a table, ordered some spiced wine, and then stared at each other for a few moments. Talah broke their silence and said, "I don't know what to think. It couldn't have been a trick. I know some of those people that were healed. I am almost speechless. Saul, tell me what you think went on."

Saul tried to process what he also had seen. He was not sure what he was going to say, for he obviously had not yet analyzed what he'd witnessed. Talah said, "Just speak from the top of your head Saul or from your heart. Just tell me what you think, as best as you can. I need your insights."

Saul began, "I witnessed miracles Talah. What is a miracle? It is the intervention of God in a person's life. Let me see if I can put this into words that are simple and logical, if that's possible." After many seconds of silence, Saul began, "Jeshua teaches that every one of us has the spirit of God inside of us. I accept this as truth. God, in his divine state, has the ability to empower people to heal themselves if his energy can reach that part of his spirit in that person that is seeking a healing.

"Most people don't have a strong enough belief or understanding of God's spirit being a part of them and how to connect God's power, to that part of God inside of them. But because of Jeshua's relationship with God and his power, he can act as a conduit between God and the people. It's not Jeshua healing them, but it is God, but it can't be done without Jeshua intervening for both of them. That's what I think took place Talah. Am I totally positive? No, but I think it's the most logical and reasonable answer I can think of right now, and I think it is the right answer. God healed those people while Jeshua prayed for them and was the conduit between God and them."

They sat in silence for a couple minutes, Talah staring into his wine goblet, and finally said, "I think you're right Saul. There is no other explanation that would make sense." The two men continued talking for awhile and then Saul rose from his chair stating that it was time for him to go.

The usual ritual of a hug goodbye was performed and then Saul turned in the direction of the upper city and began his walk home. He tried to imagine the consequences of what he witnessed. What would the reaction be of the people of Jerusalem towards Jeshua, when word got around of the healings? Surely people would revere him and adore him, and think of him as a special envoy of God. Some may literally accept him as the messiah.

The orthodox religious people and others that placed their entire faith in the clergy of the Judaic faith may have difficulty accepting these stories, feeling they are in conflict as to what the leaders of the Church teach as possible. And as for the Romans, if Jeshua's popularity grows to great proportions because of these healings, if he continues to do them, they may consider him a threat to their control over the population of Jerusalem. These were the thoughts on Saul's mind as he climbed the hill to his home as well as while he lay in bed for hours, replaying in his mind the scenes he had witnessed that day and at the well at the center of the city. Sleep came slowly, and when it did, his dreams were profound, although he couldn't remember them in the morning.

Chapter 25
Meeting at the Inn

The word spread quickly through the streets of Jerusalem. There was a man from Galilee amongst them that was performing miracles. The crippled were being given the gift of walking; the blind were being given sight, the deaf, the ability to hear. Saul heard the question being asked a hundred times, "Who is this man"?

Some of the stories being told was that he could appear or disappear at will, that he was an angel sent by God, that at times he spoke in tongues that no one could understand. When he appeared in public, crowds would follow him, asking to see miracles. So many people would come to listen to him speak, that those in the rear couldn't hear his voice.

He began to confine himself to speaking only once a week

because of the size of the crowds. Even though the Roman soldiers were not allowed inside the temple grounds, they often milled around outside of the entrances to the walls, making apparent their annoyance and displeasure of the size of the crowds and of Jeshua's activities.

Jeshua began avoiding walking the streets of the city, for crowds would follow him, begging to see a miracle. One day a message was left at one of Saul's stalls in the bazaar that Jeshua wanted to meet with him at the inn located at the intersection of the road to Bethany and Jerusalem. When Saul entered the inn at the appointed time, he found that Jeshua was already seated with another man at a table at the very rear. When Saul reached the table, Jeshua stood, and gave him a warm embrace.

"Saul, thank you for joining me. And say hello to my friend from Alexandria, Nawzad, who is passing through Judea," said Jeshua in a soft voice. Saul and the Egyptian smiled and nodded to each other, as Saul took a chair to the right of Jeshua. Jeshua continued, "Let me pour you some spiced wine that we're enjoying", remarked Jeshua, as he poured the red liquid into a pewter goblet.

Saul looked around the inn, which was very dimly lit by oil lamps sitting on some of the tables. Only one other table was occupied, because it was mid-afternoon, not the time of the day that one would generally be found in a tavern. Saul looked intently at Jeshua, their eyes meeting, and the respect and love they had for another was easily evident.

Saul then said, "Jeshua, you're making quite a stir in the city. Pretty soon you may need guards to protect you from the crowds".

Jeshua chuckled and responded, "No Saul, I have all the protection that I need from God. Whatever is meant to be will be. I know the people are confused that they think I'm the healer, but I am not". It is God that is doing the healing." not Jeshua who is God's

Nawzad then asked, "Why are some people healed and some are not?" "I'm asked that often, why it is some people are healed and some are not. That's not my decision and I truly don't know the reason why. Perhaps the one seeking the healing is so far removed from that part of God inside of them, that they are the ones preventing the healing. Or perhaps they don't believe they are capable of being healed or worthy of a healing, so they block the healing from taking place. I'm not sure, but it's not my doing.

"Saul, Nawzad is a great teller of jokes, and he travels often. What's the latest good story you have for us?" "Well, like all my stories, this one is a true one also. I was traveling across the desert from Haifa to Jerusalem by horse and I came across this man outside of the village that he lived. His name was Abdul. And he was an Arab.

He was sitting on a pile of wood and there was a line of camels to his right and some to his left lying on the ground, moaning in agony. There was one in front of him and I watched, as one at a time, he would take two very large rocks in his hands, place his hands under the camel, then place his hands on either side of the testacies of the camel, and smash them together. He was making them into eunuchs.

I was horrified, as I watched this. Finally I went up to the man and asked, 'Abdul doesn't that hurt?" He looked at me confused, and then finally answered. "No, I am fine as long as I keep my thumbs

pulled back." Saul laughed so hard his head was bent backwards. He then looked at Jeshua who was also filled with laughter. He didn't want this moment to pass. He was also consciously aware of the tremendous sense of humor that he so admired in Jeshua.

"Jeshua, I'd like to ask you a question." Saul continued, "I have known you now for almost ten years. You are what, thirty-three years old now? But you have just started doing the healing here in this province of Judea just recently. Why not earlier?" Jeshua looked at Saul, with almost sadness in his eyes, and answered, "Saul there will always be people that need to be healed, always.

"A thousand years from now there will be people that need healings. As long as people continue to contaminate their minds, their hearts and their souls by not living their lives consistent with God's will, there will be sickness and disease. I didn't begin the healings to cure humanity or to change the world. The truth is that I have traveled the three provinces of this Holy Land for many years, and have made little impact on the people. It's my messages that are important Saul, not me. And I began to ask myself, how can I get people's attention to listen to the messages, for in reality, they are not my messages, but they are God's messages and I am but the messenger.

"And one day in one of the towns along the Sea of Galilee, a man asked me to pray for him, for he was quite ill. I did pray for him and he experienced a healing. Then there was a man with a young daughter that was very ill, and I prayed for her and God healed her too. The next day when I went to preach in their small temple, the temple was totally full and people had to be turned away. And I realized that the healings could serve a very important role, by people recognizing that I am a messenger of God, shown by my praying for their healings. But there is nothing that I am doing Saul, that you also are not able to do, and someday you will."

Saul looked up at Jeshua, in great surprise. "What do you mean that I will someday be doing healings?" "You know Saul, I now have many hundreds of pupils, those that they call in Greek my disciples. And of course, there are the ones that are very close to me, the ones I originally had join me that were fishermen along the Sea of Galilee who help me with my personal needs, like John and James and Peter and, well, you've met all of them by now.

"But you are different then they are. You are not one of my disciples for a number of reasons. I speak to them in simple words, often using anecdotes, and even then I don't know if they understand the messages I am sharing. But Saul, you do understand, and always have. There is nothing I am doing that you cannot do, as well as teach the messages of God as I have been given the privilege of doing."

The three of them sat in silence for several minutes, Nawzad looking at both of them, while Jeshua and Saul looked into each other's eyes and into each other's souls. And then Jeshua said, "And there will come a time, my dear special friend from Tarsus, that indeed you will be speaking my same words, my same messages, and you will become a special messenger for God as well as for me."

Saul looked intently as Jeshua and answered, "No one can ever replace you Jeshua. I don't see that ever happening during our lifetimes." And Jeshua answered with great sadness in his voice,

"We shall see Saul. We shall see."

Chapter 26
The Parade

Many months had passed since that meeting Saul had with Jeshua in the inn on the outskirts of Jerusalem. Although Jeshua occasionally came to Jerusalem, most of this time had been spent traveling to other areas outside of the province of Judea. Saul's life continued in a routine manner, managing his investments, overseeing the retail shops he owned in the city center at the bizarre, renting the spaces to new tenants when there was turnover.

On this beautiful spring morning in mid-April we find Saul having just seated himself at a table at one of his favourite restaurants in the bazaar. Already seated was his dear friend Aaron, still heavily bearded, and still appearing as if he had spent too much time enjoying fine meals. Next to Aaron, was Shelah, the man known for his sense of humor and his enjoying dressing in a strange

attire. On this day he wore a red bandanna around his forehead, and a light weight purple robe with red circles embroidered on it.

Also at the table, was seated Nadob. His cynicism and negative outlook on matters pertaining to life had grown over the years as did his orthodox religious beliefs. There was a true bond of friendship and love among these men, who were now in their early thirties. And as for Saul, they admired his good looks without jealousy and truly respected his intelligence and financial success in life. They greeted Saul with enthusiasm as he smiled and acknowledged each of them.

"Saul, how are you handling all this excitement over Jeshua bringing Lazarus back to life after he died?" asked Aaron. "Wait a minute," exclaimed Nadob. "We don't know if Lazarus was dead or just very sick, in some sort of a coma. All we know was he was very ill for several days and then Jeshua was summoned to pray for him and now he's better. People don't return from being dead."

Aaron leaned forward towards Nadob and raised his voice, saying, "But people claim they saw him laying dead. And that by the time Jeshua arrived from Persia, or wherever he was, that the man had already died." "Saul, what have you heard?" asked Shelah, as he adjusted his bandanna.

I don't know any more than you do. And it really doesn't make a difference to me. Either way, Jeshua is Jeshua. Not too long from now he'll be leaving the home of Lazarus and his sisters and traveling from Bethany to the Temple this morning, and we've all agreed to join the crowd along the road and honor him and cheer for him. I'm sure we'll hear more information. From others who'll be there greeting him, but it will be difficult separating the truth from the rumours."

Aaron then stated, "I would think there would be greater concern of his safety, now that he's back. The rumours are that the Sanhedrin are upset at him and that the Romans are really angry at Jeshua. They are accusing him of telling people not to pay their taxes to the Romans and that we should take up weapons and rebel against them."

Saul responded, "That is ridiculous. Jeshua doesn't get involved in political issues and he doesn't believe in solving problems by using violence. As for the Sanhedrin, you have these seventy elderly men that have been appointed to their council, whose responsibility it is to help keep the people continuing to pay taxes and to not take up arms, so that the Romans don't punish and kill more of our people. They're frustrated that they have no influence over Jeshua, but they would never harm him.

"But the Romans that is something else. You know how cruel they are. They will imprison or kill people even based on rumours, or even have them crucified. They're the ones that concern me that they might injure Jeshua," Saul stated. The four men sat in silence for a few minutes, eating their breakfast, deep in their own thoughts. Then Aaron spoke up saying, "Well, in two nights from now, it will begin our Passover holiday, and Saul, we're planning your joining us for our Seder meal. My children, my parents and Zelda are looking forward to seeing you. You haven't changed your mind, have you?"

Saul answered, "Of course not Aaron. I'm looking forward to it. But right now, we better finish off our meal and head over to the road coming from Bethany. I see many people already heading that

way. I don't want to miss it."

Shela asked, "What influence does the Sanhedrin have over the Romans and Pontius Pilate?" Aaron answered, "They don't have any influence. The Romans could care less what any Jew has to say, let alone the Sanhedrin. Can you even imagine Pilate asking the Sanhedrin for advice?" Saul began to raise from the table. "We better get going so we're not late. We have a long walk ahead of us to get to the road from Bethany"

The four friends left the restaurant area and began to walk through the bazaar among the hundreds of shops in an easterly direction. The bazaar wasn't crowded this time of the morning and they didn't want to appear in a great hurry so that they wouldn't be detained by any Roman soldiers they may encounter, that would stop them and question them. They exited the bazaar by going past the Pool of Siloam and then through the Water Gate until they reached the dirt road which took them in a northerly direction.

They walked past the Spring of Gihon on their right, which was the source of water for the Pool of Siloam. Saul always enjoyed taking this route, for it was quiet and he could enjoy the beautiful landscaping that had been planted on both sides of the spring, and to his right he could see the mountains which formed the Kidron Valley. The men continued their light conversation, making sure they didn't walk faster than necessary so Aaron could keep up, and eventually they passed the pinnacle of the Temple on their left which was the southeast corner of the walls that surrounded the magnificent Temple. In spite of Saul now having lived in Jerusalem for ten years, he never got over the extraordinary beauty of the Temple with its huge pillars and its enormous size.

The road soon turned abruptly due north, and after a few minutes they passed the Garden of Gethsemane on their left, which was located in a very popular park about a ten minute walk east of the Temple walls. And now as they approached the road from Bethany, they could see hundreds of people had already lined themselves on both sides of the road. The people were in a festive mood, laughing and shouting out to friends standing on the other side of the road. Unlike the profile of those who generally were found at Jeshua's sermons, there were many young people, women and children that were among the crowd.

Saul and his three friends crossed the road and found a place in the crowd in which they were in the third row of people, but behind a large group of youngsters so they could easily see over their heads. Every so often someone would begin to shout Jeshua's name, and hundreds would join in, "Jeshua, Jeshua, Jeshua," they chanted. And soon the air was filed with excitement, as people were shouting, "He's coming. He's coming".

The men looked down the road to their left, and indeed they could see Jeshua approaching them, still several minutes away. He was traveling very slowly, sitting astride of a gray donkey. He was wearing a light gray robe that blended in with the color of the donkey, and when he got within about fifty yards of where Saul was standing, they could see that Jeshua had a huge smile on his face. The crowd on either side were throwing flowers at Jeshua, as he continued laughing, smiling and waving at them.

As he reached the point where the three men were standing,

Jeshua looked at them and Saul and Jeshua made eye contact. It appeared to Saul as if for a moment, a sadness almost passed across Jeshua's face, and he had stopped smiling when their eyes met. Saul held up his right hand in greeting, palm facing Jeshua and Jeshua did the same to Saul. Saul felt as if he was in vacuum. As if the people around him had frozen as well as their sounds had been muted. It was almost as if Jeshua was now moving along the road on the donkey in slow motion.

"What in the world is going on", Saul thought to himself, as Jeshua slowly went past him. As Jeshua passed people, they would step out onto the road and flow behind him as if in a parade, so that the process now consisted of hundreds of people walking behind Jeshua and the donkey he was riding. But Saul and his comrades held their ground, and soon they were looking at the backs of the many that were following him. Talah then spoke, "Wow, that was some sight. Look at the thousands of flowers on the road. Nadob, you should pick them and open a flower shop and sell them at the bazaar." "Yes, responded Nadob, "And you should get a job cleaning up the droppings of the donkeys and horses and camels that are left on the road between Bethany and Jerusalem."

The four men followed the crowd which eventually passed the Pool of Bethesda on their right, and then the jail and Antonio Fortress appeared to their left that was located on the northwest corner of the outside of the Temple walls. The people of Jerusalem hated this fortress for it was here that the Roman soldiers would imprison Jews and interrogate them, beat them and leave them in the jail as prisoners.

They soon came to the entrance and walked through the West Gate into the Temple grounds, where people had gathered to hear Jeshua speak from the stairs of the Portico. But the crowd was immense, and Saul and his friends were so far back, that they couldn't hear any words that Jeshua would have spoken, so they agreed to leave the Temple grounds and go their respective ways. Saul, traveling by himself, made his way east past the Praetorium, and then south towards the upper city, in the direction where he lived. As he entered the gate to the upper city he could see Herod's Palace to his right, commanding a site that had a view overlooking the entire city of Jerusalem.

Saul was having trouble concentrating. He couldn't maintain his thoughts or control the uncomfortable feeling inside of him. He felt that his anxiety was being caused because of deep concerns he had inside himself over the safety of Jeshua. As he continued his walk to his home he prayed silently for Jeshua's well being. Then his thoughts turned to the holiday he would be celebrating two days from now, and the Seder ceremony he would be attending at the home of his friend, Aaron. Passover, he thought, was a time to celebrate, not a time to be filled with worry.

Chapter 27
The Seder

Two days had passed since Saul had witnessed Jeshua riding the donkey on the road from Bethany to Jerusalem. It was now dusk, the time of the day when late afternoon trades its place with the early hours of the evening. We find Saul in his room carefully selecting the clothes he would wear while attending the important Passover services at his friend Aaron's home.

The Passover holiday is in memory of a time going back over a thousand years before Saul was born. The Jewish people had lived in peace for many years in the eastern part of the Nile Delta in Egypt until a new Pharaoh decided to enslave the Jews and forced them to build two new cities that were to be the centers of food supplies for the Egyptians.

In order to convince the Pharaoh to release the Jews from slavery,

plagues were brought by God against the Egyptian people. After refusing to release them following the first nine plagues, the tenth plague brought widespread suffering and uproar resulting in the Pharaoh freeing the slaves and demanding that they immediately leave Egypt. It is that tenth plague which created the name of the holiday being known as Passover.

The Jews had been told to place the blood of a lamb on the door jamb of the entrance into their homes and that the angel of death would "Passover" their homes but would enter those of the Egyptians and bring death to the first born son of each Egyptian family.

The Passover holiday is celebrated for eight days and always begins on the 15th day of the Hebrew month of Nisan, and the first evening being the most important event of the holiday. It as on this night, in almost every Jewish home in the world that they would be having a Seder, which is an exactly prescribed ritual held during the evening dinner. This is a ritual that will continue forever as long as there are people in the world who still observe the Jewish religion.

Saul chose his clothes for comfort, knowing he would sitting at the table for many hours. He selected a white tunic that came just below his knees, and soft sandals with only one connecting strap, rather than the stiffer ones designed for walking long distances. The sleeves of his tunic fell just below his elbows. With his tanned face, black wavy hair, short beard and green eyes, he looked radiant dressed in his holiday attire.

When Saul arrived at the home of Aaron, he was greeted at the door by Aaron's wife Zelda. "Well look at you," exclaimed Zelda.

"I'd better hide all the women." "The only woman I want is the one in front of me right now", Saul responded as he reached out and grabbed Zelda, drawing her towards him in a big hug. Zelda squealed in delight as she hugged Saul back.

Saul was led into the large family room where two long wooden tables had been placed side by side. Most of the people were already seated and were relatives as well as the two children of Zelda and Aaron who were approaching their teenage years. Also, seated at the head of the table was Aaron's father Abrahim, who was a slightly larger version of Aaron, but with a white beard surrounding his large round face.

The youngest son of Aaron would be asking his grandfather Mah Nishtanah, which means the four questions that are asked of the family patriarch as to why this night was different than any other night. The answers to the each question describe specific events of the Passover story and the symbolic meaning of those events.

Saul was seated in the middle of the table between two females' cousins of Aaron, who Saul liked but had never had a romantic interest in either, much to the dismay of the young ladies. Wine had begun to be drunk by the adults and conversation was plentiful. Abrahim leaned forward and asked, "Saul, were you with Aaron watching your friend, Jeshua, ride his donkey into Jerusalem?"

"Yes I was, Abrahim. It was quite a sight." "So what's your opinion? Have you heard, was Lazarus dead or was he just very ill?" asked Abrahim. Saul spent a few moments in deep thought. He couldn't get out of his mind the sad look in Jeshua's eyes as they made contact with one another. Something inside Saul's mind was

unsettled, as if he was beginning to feel some unexplained anxiety. "I really don't know if he was dead or not, and frankly, it doesn't make a difference to me. Either way, it doesn't change who Jeshua is."

An aunt of Aaron's then asked, "And who is Jeshua to you Saul?" Saul didn't answer, and after awhile Aaron broke the silence by asking, "Saul, where is Jeshua tonight?" Saul answered, "He's celebrating the Seder at the home of Zebedee, who's the father of the two fishermen, John and James, who are two of Jeshua's pupils. Zebedee owns a fleet of fishing boats on the Sea of Galilee and has a large older home here, in the upper city, not too far from the Temple."

"After what happened two days ago, I'll bet there's quite a crowd there," remarked Zelda. Saul responded, "Probably so. I know from the Magdalene family, only Mary will be there. Martha will stay home taking care of Lazarus. Zebedee has some fine cooks. I'm sure it will be quite a supper."

"Well, we're going to have a great one ourselves", commented Abrahim. "Is everything in place, the matzoh, the food, the bitter herbs, and of course, the wine?"

The wine during the ceremony was a special wine, like a desert wine, much sweeter than a normal drinking wine. There would be a time during the ceremony that Abrahim, as the patriarch, would take a sip of the wine and then pass his goblet from person to person, each one taking a sip from the goblet.

The first of the four questions asked by Aaron's youngest son was, "Why is it that on all other nights during the year we eat either bread or matzoh. But on this night we eat only matzoh?" Abrahim's answer was, "We eat only matzoh because our ancestors could not wait for their breads to rise when they were fleeing slavery in Egypt, and so they took the bread out of their ovens while they were still flat, which was matzoh,"

Abarhim then took a large piece of matzoh, the unleavened bread, and broke off a piece to eat and passed it around the table for each person to do the same. These rituals represented the sharing that the Jews that had left slavery had to do to survive the many years they traveled through the desert, looking for their new homeland.

The main course consisted of roasted lamb with plenty of fresh cooked vegetables. Much wine was drunk and the conversation following the ceremony was lively. Saul's mind kept wandering, trying to envision what was taking place with Jeshua and all the others at Zebedee's home. Saul had been invited there, but he felt he would be more comfortable being at Aaron's home, which is where he had spent the last six Passover Seders.

He thought of those past years when he used to bring Leah with him, and he felt an emptiness in his heart, a void he could not fill. His mind kept wandering back and forth between Leah and Jeshua, and he concluded the sadness he felt inside of him was probably for his longing for Leah, a woman he had given up, but not his love for her.

When his thoughts transferred from Leah to Jeshua, he would think of the healings he had witnessed, the sermons he had heard, and the sight of Jeshua riding the donkey into Jerusalem, between the large crowds along the roadway, and the sadness his saw in his

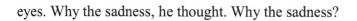

eyes. Why the sadness, he thought. Why the sadness?

Chapter 28
The Crucifixion

Saul was fast asleep, when he thought he heard his name being called. He struggled to open his eyes and clear his mind. "Saul, wake up. Saul, get up. It's me, Jocelyn." The voice was that of a woman, sobbing very deeply, as if in great anguish. He wasn't sure if he was dreaming or if he was hearing the voice of his landlord. He had drunk a substantial amount of wine the night before at the Passover Seder, which was very unusual for him, and he had gone to bed very late. But through the fog of his mind, his instincts were starting to come to life as he heard the continued plea for him to awaken.

"Saul, please. You must get up. I have horrible news for you," said the almost hysterical voice, fighting through the crying. Saul sat up in his bed, wiping the sleep from his eyes, and saw at the foot of his bed was the matronly form of Jocelyn, who along with her

husband were his landlords. "What is it Jocelyn? What's going on?" he asked with a cold dreading feeling entering his body.

Her words fought through the almost uncontrollable crying. "They have killed him, Saul. Jeshua is dead. The Romans crucified him this morning." Saul froze as if he was paralyzed. His mind processed what he heard and then a loud shrieking voice escaped from his throat. "Nooooooo", he screamed. He began to cry uncontrollably. His body heaving from the pain and agony he felt inside of him. He lost all sense of time and where he was. His mind had become a vacuum, as he fought through the confusion trying to think of what he could do, what he should do.

Finally after many minutes had gone by, he realized he was alone in his room. He got out of bed, and without conscious thought, he began to dress himself. He tried to think of what he was going to do next, but in the recess of his mind, he knew he was in shock. When he finished dressing, he went in the kitchen and found Joselyn with her face lying on the table, softly crying. She looked up when she realized he had entered the room, and forced herself to speak. "I am so sorry Saul. I am so sorry. God help us. I am so sorry."

Saul turned and exited the kitchen, into the hallway and went out the front door. He began to walk toward the road in front of the house and make his way down the hill of the upper city, towards the center of the city. He had no idea where he was going, and he made his way out of habit. Every so often, he would stop and buckle over in pain, a pain that seemed to envelope his heart, so deep, so intense, that he could barely breathe. Every so often a huge sob would escape his throat, and the word "Noooo" could be heard in an almost inhuman tone, as if emanating from a wounded animal.

He did not know how he got there or how long it took him, but he found himself now walking through the bazaar toward the lower city. If he had passed people he knew, he wasn't aware of their presence. He could see people milling around the bazaar, but there was an eerie silence surrounding him. He didn't know if the silence was real or if he had created it, but he could feel a stillness around him, as if people were walking in slow motion, in trances, as if the world around him had entered a different dimension, one that was heavy with grief and agony.

Saul looked up and realized he had found his way to the home of Thomas, whose modest house in the lower city he had last visited years ago. Thomas was one of Jeshua's close pupils. Perhaps he could tell Saul what had happened. One part of him said it doesn't matter.

'My brother, the man I love more than anybody else in the world is gone.' Another part of him was hoping that Jocelyn was wrong, and that Thomas would tell him that Jeshua was still alive. He didn't think these thoughts consciously. He realized he was in some sort of a stupor, acting by instinct rather than thought.

He pounded on the door of the house, and as soon as Thomas opened the door, he knew the truth, Jeshua was dead, no longer with them. He had been killed by the Romans. Thomas' eyes were swollen from the tears he had shed. His pain was visible on his face. Thomas turned and walked towards the kitchen and sat down at on the wooden seat facing Saul. Saul closed the front door and slowly followed him, and sat down in the wooden chair opposite him. They looked at each other in silence for a few minutes, and then Thomas spoke. *Jeshua's death*

"Saul, I will tell you all that I know. I know how much you loved him". Thomas bowed his head for over a minute, as if trying to collect his thoughts as he sifted through his memory. And then spoke, in a soft voice, in control but in obvious pain.

"Last night we had our Seder at the home of Zebedee. Even though he wasn't the oldest, Jeshua sat at the head of the table and acted as the patriarch. There were eighteen of us sitting around the long table with Mary sitting next to Jeshua. There were also three of the wives seated with us. There was another large table set upstairs where others were also having the Seder. Jeshua was his usual self, filled with wisdom and humor." Thomas stopped for awhile, as if he was trying to grasp the facts in a logical order. Saul absorbed every word he was hearing, trying to visualize what had taken place.

Thomas continued, "The ceremony was over late in the evening. Jeshua suggested that we walk over to the Garden of Gethsemane, and spend the night sleeping in the park. It was a pleasant night out, and so a group of us headed towards Gethsemane, only the men.

"When we got there, we separated in small groups, finding a comfortable place to sleep for the night. I have no idea how much time went by, for I was fast asleep, and then I heard this great commotion.

"People were shouting, and when I woke up, I saw that there were many Roman soldiers with their swords drawn. Two of them had surrounded him, holding him by his arms, but he didn't resist. We shouted at them demanding to know what they were doing. They wouldn't answer, just threatening us not to interfere. Then they took him away. We followed them at a distance. They took Jeshua to the jail at Antonio Fortress."

Thomas got up from his seat. He began to pace back and forth in the small kitchen area. His eyes were dazed but steady, and it appeared to Saul he was deep in thought, trying to remember every detail. Saul still did not speak, not wanting to interfere with the concentration of Thomas. Although his head was still throbbing, and he was still overwhelmed with grief, he was now able to begin thinking clearer, as he envisioned all that Thomas was sharing.

Then Thomas continued, "We waited through the night until the sun came up, hoping they would release Jeshua. Eventually some men came out of the Praetorium located just east of the jail and we ran to them. They weren't soldiers but Romans that were employed by them, taking care of their administrative needs. They tried to tell us that the Sanhedrin had met in the middle of the night after Jeshua had been arrested and they had a trial for him and had found him guilty of blasphemy and in violation of Roman laws.

"We knew this was lie. The Sanhedrin are seventy elderly men scattered around the city. There would be no reason for them to meet in the middle of the night. If they wanted to meet they would have met this morning. Also it's not their function to hold a trial for a person for their main duties are the training and supervision of the priests and the temples. I have a friend whose father is a member of the Sanhedrin and he told me later that the Sanhedrin had no knowledge that Jeshua had been arrested and then crucified until after it had been done.

"We asked where Jeshua was now. It was then that they told us that Pilate had ordered him to be crucified, in place of one of the three others that that they had planned to kill that morning."

Thomas began to cry and wail, with the speaking of those words. Saul also began to sob, but still remained silent, wanting Thomas to continue. "Not too long afterwards, they brought Jeshua out, flanked by soldiers on either side. He was bleeding all over his back and chest, and they had placed a crown of thorns on his head. They placed on his shoulders a long heavy board, and began to walk him from the Prateorium to Golgotha, where the crucifixions take place. There were very few people along the streets from the Preatorium to Golgotha, for it was still early morning, and people would be just getting up from their sleep, after having the Seder last night.

"But those that saw what was going on were in shock. They began crying and some screamed out the words 'murderers' and 'killers' at the Roman soldiers. But the Roman soldiers warned them not to interfere or they would also be arrested. They also warned us to leave or we would be accused of the same crimes that Jeshua had been accused of and been found guilty of doing.

"Then Saul," Thomas said in a raised voice filled with anger and pain. "They killed him. They put a sign in Latin in front of him that read 'King of the Jews' and they crucified him. They killed our beloved Jeshua," Thomas moaned as he walked towards Saul, who was now standing, and buried his face on his shoulder, his body heaving with spasms of grief.

As the two men hugged each other, Saul also began to quietly weep. Saul spent about another hour with Thomas, both men trying to console each other, but with no success. They both agreed that the reason Jeshua had been arrested by the Romans at night rather than during daytime, was to avoid a mob reaction by his many followers. And they wanted to crucify him in the early morning knowing that very few people would know until it was too late, in order to avoid possible rioting.

After Thomas told Saul he had no more information to share, Saul left his house, heading back towards the bazaar and the upper city. He had no interest of going to Golgatha, for he assumed by now Jeshua had been removed from the cross. Also he would not have been able to bear seeing his beloved friend in pain, suffering on the cross. Right now, he just wanted to be alone. He didn't want to talk to anyone or see anyone.

He wanted to be alone with his thoughts and his emotions and his memories. He went back to his house and filled two large sacks with some food, a blanket and some other supplies. He then headed eastward, towards the Jordan River into the uninhabited land, where he would spend the next few days, grieving, in mourning and in solitude, asking God for explanations, and honoring the memory of the man whom he loved beyond words.

CHAPTER 29
The Road to Damascus

Following the death of Jeshua, Saul preferred spending most of his time without the companionship of others. He found solace in revisiting the memories of days gone by as he walked the hill country outside of the walls of the city. He thought about his youth, running after the sheep in the fields of his father's estate outside of Tarsus.

He thought of his father, Zerah, a man that did not know how to show affection, and he wished he had been able to have been closer to him. He thought of his mother, her timid behavior and her constant concern over upsetting his father. Both of his parents had now passed on, and his memories were vivid, as if they were still in their younger years.

Saul had very fond memories of the tutors he had, that had shared with him their knowledge and wisdom. They were a substitution for the friends he wasn't allowed to have as a youth growing up. And they too were vivid in his mind, as if they had not aged a day since he last saw them. He preferred remembering them as they were, and not as they probably were at this time, if indeed, if any were still alive.

He thought of the ocean voyage he had taken across the Great Sea, to the Holy land. He relived the memories of the lady friends he had over the years and he spent many hours pretending he had made different decisions in that regard. In his mind he allowed himself to have married Leah, and he visualized the home they would have had in the upper city, and the children they would have been raising. In his mind's imagination, he watched them as they played with the children of his friends, Aaron, Talah, Shaleh and Nadob. He watched them grow to teen years, as he and Leah lived a life of quiet luxury.

But when it came time to transfer his thoughts to the memories of Jeshua, he experienced great pain. Every thought of Jeshua touched a sensitive place in his heart that was almost unbearable. He wondered if the agony inside of him would subside with time. He longed for the day he could think of Jeshua with love and not have it accompanied by the grief.

Many things were transpiring in Judea since Jeshua's death. About a week after Jeshua's death, Saul had wandered down to the lower city and ran into Cephas, the man who was also called Peter by some of the others. Cephas was very excited as he tried to tell Saul that Jeshua had appeared to them after his death. That he had supped with them and that he told them he wanted them to carry on with his teachings, and that he, Peter would become one of the new leaders. But now Jeshua was gone again.

Saul didn't know what to make of this story. He had never been close to Peter and had always thought of him as boisterous and argumentative. Did it really happen, or was it self-serving to Jeshua's followers? But either way, he didn't care. It didn't change who Jeshua was to him any more than whether Lazarus had been raised from death by Jeshua or recovered from a deep sickness of unconsciousness.

Many months will have passed by. Jeshua's pupils and followers, those that they called disciples, established an organization that they called The Witnesses. They created a headquarters in a two story house in Bethany, not too far from the home of the Magdalenes. They now referred to themselves as the teachers of the knowledge of Jeshua which they called the Good News. They adopted the Greek name of the word teachers, so called themselves apostles.

When Saul had heard that they had appointed Jeshua's brother James as the figure head leader of their group, Saul felt contempt towards them. James had never been supportive of Jeshua's activities and for them to now make him their pretend leader was an insult to the memory of Jeshua. He assumed they did this to try to establish some credibility.

One afternoon three of the apostles paid a visit to Saul at his home. Saul greeted them outside and they sat on benches on either side of a wooden table, with a view looking down to the lower city and the marketplace. John was the spokesman for the three men.

"We've been discussing you at our meetings Saul. We've now appointed a total of seventy people as the new apostles, just as the Sanhedrin have seventy men. We've developed rules and regulations and you could be a great help to us with your background and education."

Saul responded quietly, "I have heard your rules and regulations John. You're recruiting many people over the three provinces and inviting them to become members of your organization, but you're requiring them to donate all of their wealth to your group. And I have two problems, major problems, with the actions of The Witnesses." "And what are your concerns Saul?" asked John.

Saul answered, "You're telling these people that God is going to punish them if they don't give you one hundred per cent of all their assets, and then become a member of your community. Jeshua would never have condoned your threatening people that God would punish them. And hasn't it occurred to you that some of the people that are joining your organization are only doing so that they may receive free food and shelter without having to work? That they could care less for the teachings of Jeshua and are only interested in the free benefits of living in the commune?"

No matter what arguments they gave to support their actions, Saul would not budge. They didn't leave in hostility. Each wished the other well, acknowledging the bond they had through the love they all carried for Jeshua. Saul did make some suggestions to them, but he knew they would discard them as soon as they left the property.

Over the next several years Saul concentrated on his business activities. He had purchased several more stalls at the bazaar and had hired an individual to manage them for him. He had also begun to apply his business knowledge in other areas. He would purchase a very large parcel of land, and then divide into five or six smaller parcels.

He would then lease out the land to tenant farmers, some who raised animals on their portion of the rented land and others that would grow products to sell in the market place. These actions were very financially lucrative but Saul didn't enter into these activities to accumulate more wealth for himself. He did it to occupy his mind. In fact, most of his newly created wealth, he gave way anonymously to charities, to help widows and orphaned children.

The summer months had just passed when Saul received an invitation from some businessmen he had met in Jerusalem that lived in Damascus, Syria. They knew of the success Saul was experiencing in Judea buying large parcels of and dividing them into smaller ones and then leasing them out. They felt there were many opportunities to do the same in the Damascus area and wanted Saul to join them as a partner. Saul accepted their invitation and began to make plans for the journey to Damascus.

Damascus was 140 miles from Jerusalem, through barren desert land. It was a trip that generally took two weeks and required careful preparation and planning. There were companies that offered to chaperone people for a price from one location to the other. They would provide the camel to ride, two guides that had been trained to protect against thieves, cook the food for their meals and assure safe passage. They knew the distances between each oasis and how to time their arrivals.

There were three other men besides Saul that showed up at the location they were told to meet to begin their trip, along with the two guides that were both Bedouin Arabs. Each of the six were assigned a camel and there was a seventh camel that carried the provisions for the trip. It was early morning and after introductions, one of the guides, Jamul, explained the journey, how long it would take and what they could expect along the way.

The men reached the first oasis in the early afternoon and stopped to eat lunch and give the camels an opportunity to replenish themselves. While sitting around the campfire in a circle, one of them, a heavy set man from Jerusalem, turned to Saul and asked, "You look familiar. Have I seen you at the Temple listening to the preacher from Galilee a few years ago?"

"Yes, I've been there" Saul answered. "So, what do you think?" continued the man. "Why did the Romans kill him?" One of the other men, a small thin man with a pointed beard spoke up. "There's nothing to think about. He had huge crowds following him around. The Romans claimed he was trying to get the people to take up arms against them. He became a threat to them. You know the Romans; they kill the Jews and ask questions afterwards."

The first man spoke, "Some say that the Sanhedrin asked the Romans to kill him." "Camel dung," the small man responded. "Jews don't kill their own. Besides, you think the Romans care what the Jews want or don't want?" The third man then spoke up. "I'm from Damascus, on my way back to my home. What we hear in Damascus is that there are people in my city that would like to join the Brotherhood, or the Witnesses, whatever they call themselves, but they won't let them unless they convert to your religion."

"Then why don't they convert?" asked the heavy set man. The Syrian responded, "To join, they have to get circumcised, agree to eat your special food and learn the rules and rituals of your religion. Would you want your zayin cut off at your age, and also have to stop eating your favorite food? Anyway, most of them can't read anyway. How are they going to learn all your customs?"

Saul listened to their conversations, which would continue through the many days they traveled through the barren desert. Sometimes he was amused, other times he found their words annoying and would remove himself from the circle and walk away from the campfire, into the desert to be alone with his private thoughts. He never participated in their discussions and they recognized he didn't want to socialize with them, even though he was always courteous and polite towards them.

On the fourteenth day of their journey, they reached Kakae, the last oasis before arriving at the gated walls of Damascus. Jamul, the Bedouin leader of the small caravan turned to them and said, "It's getting late, and when you reach the gates of the city you have to pay a toll to get in. But at night the gates are closed because of the darkness, so you have to wait until sunrise to pay the toll and enter. So we'll camp here tonight, at this last oasis and leave early in the morning. It will be about a half day ride to get there."

The men dismantled, and led their camels to the well so the Arabs could water them. A fire was then built at the campfire, and the guides began to cook their dinner. The men were tired from the two weeks they had been traveling through the desert, and there was very

little conversation. Following their meal, they prepared themselves for sleep, for they would be waking up early the next morning to complete their journey.

As usual, Saul made his bedding further away from the others, so he wouldn't hear their late conversations or their snoring while they slept. He lay on his back with his eyes open, looking at the thousands of stars in the sky. There was a very slight breeze but the weather was comfortable, and after awhile his mind brushed aside his thoughts and memories and he fell asleep.

Saul didn't know how much time had gone by, but he woke with a sudden movement of his body, and he found himself wide awake. A strange feeling encompassed him, almost as if he was engulfed in a blanket of indescribable emotion. He felt compelled to rise from his bedding, and he began to walk further from the campsite, into the desert. And then he saw the light. Directly in front of him was a circle of light and to his absolute astonishment a man was seated in the middle of the light on the desert floor. As he approached the light, he fell to his knees, as he realized the man was Jeshua.

Saul rose to his feet and slowly walked to within several feet of the light, his eyes squinting because of the brilliance of the light, and he was mesmerized at the sight of the man he loved more than life itself. Jeshua was looking directly at Saul, in total silence, as Saul returned to his knees.

After some time had passed is silence, Saul said in a whisper, "Jeshua, Jeshua, I miss you so much," tears flowing down his cheeks, as he sobbed uncontrollably. Jeshua finally spoke, his melodious voice that Saul knew breaking the silence. "My dear brother, I come to you with love. I know what is in your heart and the agony that you feel within. I am going to make a request of you Saul, one which you may choose to accept or reject. It is a request, should you accept, that will totally change your life.

"I am asking that you take the teachings that I have shared with you, and that you become my voice, my messenger of the truth. That you become the apostle of my words, which are God's words. If you accept, you will revert back to your Roman name of Paul, for you will be traveling for many years throughout the empire, many times in hostile places, where you will need the protection of your Roman citizenship. But even then, you will be exposed to many hardships, even beatings and sometimes imprisonment.

"But you will impact the lives of the masses. You will become the vehicle for Divine Intent. Your voice will be heard throughout this world. And your voice will become the instrument through which the Truth is destined to pass. The Truth you will come to bear unto this world is not yours. But ultimately, you will become that Truth.

"Your mission will change the future of humanity, but the mission is not yours. It is God's. And you will not be honored with glory while you live and you will spend your last years of your life alone, in the custody of others outside of the Holy Land. The commitment you are being asked to make is a difficult one. It is not a demand, my beloved brother, but a request. You may take as long as you need to make the decision, and you will always be loved by me, no matter which way you decide."

Saul bowed his head. He felt as if some miracle had made an

opening in his heart, and out poured all the agony, all the anguish, all the pain that had been contained within him since the death of Jeshua. His being was filled with an ecstasy of joy, and of understanding and of bliss.

Only a short time went by in silence, and then Paul raised his head, looking directly into the light, in spite of its brilliance, the tears still flowing, and said, "I accept this mission Jeshua. I will be your messenger. Yes, I am making this commitment."

AFTERWORD

The Roman Catholic Church was created in the fourth century by the Emperor Constantine. I have written about those events in great detail in my book, *Time for Truth* that was published in September of 2010. There were a number of areas in which the leaders of the new Church chose to give a different interpretation than the facts support. I would like to address some of them at this time, which deals with the title of this book, *The Commitment.*

In the teachings of the Church they try to portray Paul as a person who prosecuted and caused harm to the followers of Jeshua after his death. They then claim that Paul decided to travel to Damascus, Syria to arrest Syrian Jews who had accepted Jeshua as their spiritual leader.

They continue their fictitious account of the truth by them claiming that on the way to Damascus Jeshua appeared to Paul in the desert and Paul made a conversion to Christianity. Let's explore these extraordinary declarations of the Church which are still being taught today.

Paul was not in a position of authority to persecute Jews who had accepted Jeshua as their messiah or spiritual leader. He was a businessman. Now would he have had any reason to persecute them, for he was totally dedicated to the teachings of Jeshua. That was why he was able to travel throughout the Roman Empire forming churches and teaching the messages of Jeshua after Jeshua died.

He knew those messages and teachings of Jeshua better than any other living person, then or now. This is a fact, and also logic dic-

tates that he could not have known the teachings of Jeshua if he had not had the loving and intimate relationship with Jeshua while they both lived, as I have described in my book. This is totally contrary to the Church claiming they did not know each other and that Paul wanted to persecute his followers.

As you now know, the reason Paul is not mentioned in the gospels is because Paul was not a disciple. There was no reason for the three disciples who wrote three of the four gospels to mention him for he was not one of them. The fourth gospel writer, Luke, was not a disciple, but was a Greek citizen who met Paul on one of his missions and wrote about Paul in great detail in Acts in the New Testament.

As for the Church claiming Paul traveled to Syria to arrest Syrian Jews because they had accepted the teachings of Jeshua, let us examine that likelihood. Paul would have had to travel 140 miles across the desert from Jerusalem to Damascus, locate these Syrian Jews, and take them under arrest. Let us assume he is going to arrest four of them he selected out of random. With his weapon of a sword, he would somehow take these four men as his prisoners, chain them, and get them past the guards at the gates. He then would have to travel two weeks through the desert with them, provide each of them with their own camel, feed them, take care of their bodily needs, and then bring them into Jerusalem to be arrested.

Arrested for what? Having accepted the teachings of Jeshua? There were hundreds of Jews in Jerusalem that had accepted the teachings of Jeshua and none of them had been prosecuted or arrested by the Romans in Jerusalem. In reality, had Paul tried to do such an absurd thing in Syria, he would have been immediately killed or sent to a prison for the insane.

Now let us examine the assertion by the Church, which I have heard preached hundreds of times in Church services, that Paul made a conversion on the Road to Damascus. A conversion to what? The only religion that existed in the Holy Land was Judaism. There was nothing to convert to. The Church wants us to believe that he converted to Christianity. But it was Paul that founded Christianity four years later, when he found that there were people throughout the Roman Empire that wanted to accept Jeshua's teachings but did not qualify to become members of the Jewish religion, for the reasons I explained in my book. They did not want to be circumcised, change what foods they could eat or study and learn the details of the Jewish religion.

No, there was no conversion; there was a "commitment". And that is why I chose to call my book *The Commitment* and that is why my subtitle is *The True Story*. And now you do have the true story. Thank you for allowing me to share with you.

God bless you as you continue on your journey.

Nick Bunick

CONTACT THE AUTHOR

When *The Messengers* came out in 1997, we provided an address for people to write to us, and we also listed phone numbers. This created a problem, for we received more than 10,000 letters in the first six months, and it was impossible to respond to everybody. Of those we did respond to, many began to write to us on a regular basis, which created an even greater logjam. My staff and I felt bad that we couldn't answer all of the mail. The same is true of the phone calls—we had four lines that were constantly jammed.

For those reasons, we've decided that instead of a mailing address and phone numbers, we would provide a website in order for you to reach us:

www.nickbunick.com

Our site is an interactive site in that it is both a chat site and a blog. We have people from all over the world communicating with me and to each other regarding many spiritual issues and topics. On our site there is a place for the media to click for TV and radio interview requests, talk-show invitations, and magazine and newspaper features. We will make every effort to reply to inquiries within 24 hours.

We'll also keep you posted as to when and where I will be doing speaking engagements. There are channeled messages from Jeshua and Mother Mary. There are radio interviews that I have had that you can listen to. There are the vows that spirit has provided us to

live by that of tremendous benefit. There are many other spiritual activities happening on our site that you will enjoy reading and will hopefully participate in.

Come and join us to help foster universal compassion and universal love around the world. We welcome your ideas and there are many changes that must be brought about, but with your help, I know we can be successful.

Love and blessings to each of you.

Nick Bunick

Acknowledgements

The Commitment has been self-published so it did not have the benefit of professional editors that are used in publishing companies. But perhaps of even greater value to me, I had the editorial help of several talented and dedicated people that enabled me to have their constant feedback through e-mail communication with them on a regular basis. They were fantastic.

I first want to thank Bill Hawkins for the tremendous job he did and the help he gave me. His technical skills provided me the ability to work with the manuscript and its production that I never could have done by myself. And he was always there to encourage me, to offer suggestions and constantly looking at ways to improve our book. Bill wore so many hats in his helping me; he must have at least fifty heads.

In addition to Bill, I received great support from Barbara Bell and Miryana Brkic (Ulic)..............Barbara is a tigress, and often times insisted I include something I was reluctant to do, until she also made me a believer. And Miryana, all the way from Australia…her talent, her insights, her suggestions were tremendously helpful and indeed, influenced our finished product.

There is another group that I want to acknowledge that are too many to mention. These are my spiritual colleagues that I sometimes refer to as my soul mates that meet me almost daily on my website, nickbunick.com. You know who you are. You inspired me, you

motivated me, you gently pushed me, and you gave me the love and support that I shall always be grateful for.

I dedicate this book to all of you above…and to the millions of others in the world who love and respect Jeshua and who are seekers of the truth.

Nick Bunick

OTHER BOOKS BY NICK BUNICK

The Messengers........In 1997 this book took the country by storm and became an instant New York Times best seller. The authors were Gary Hardin and Nick Bunick. He was the subject of this amazing book that impacted the lives of over a million people.

The first half of this book tells of the incredible miracles that happened in Nick's life, which placed him on the path he is on today. The second half of this extraordinary book is the fascinating transcription of the tapes when Nick was hypnotized and taken back 2000 years ago to the lifetime of Paul.........This book will have a major impact in your life............

In God's Truth.....This book was written by Nick describing the amazing events in his life that happened after the publishing of *The Messengers*. It provides you the truth and evidence of the role that your angels and spirit guides play in your life. It gives you insights into the understanding of our souls and proof as well as the history of reincarnation. This book will help you understand your relationship with God and enhance your own spirituality as well to understand there is no such thing as death. You will experience a healing of your own spirit and soul.

Time for Truth....A New Beginning......This miraculous book is destined to change your life as well as the world as we know it today. It has been written for you and everybody else

on Earth who is interested in the truth and a new beginning. *This book* will take you on an incredible journey. It also presents you with the true story of what happened.

Two thousand years ago, revealing how messages of compassion and love were turned into teachings of guilt and fear. Along the way you will be given a new and profound understanding of the spiritual world and the purpose of your life. This book is the pathway to transformation and enlightenment and a new beginning.

Book prices:

The Messengers.................................$15.00

In God's Truth $12.00

Time for Truth....A New Beginning.........$15.00

*Please add $5.00 for each title ordered for shipping and handling.

Order books by sending a check in USA funds to:

Skywin,

P.O. Box 2222

Lake Oswego, Oregon 97035

or through amazon.com or your local book stores

*Please note that all prices are in USA dollars

Made in the USA
Middletown, DE
08 October 2020